YOUR EARS
AREN'T THAT BIG

Your Ears Aren't THAT Big

ROSA VALLE-LOPEZ

WordPaddle

Los Angeles

Cover Design by Summer Verwers. Cover Illustration by Flora Valle. Cover original photograph by Prabin Basnet. Author photograph by Tony Buttitta Photography.

ISBN: 979-8-9899110-1-1 (print)
ISBN: 979-8-9899110-0-4 (ebook)
Library of Congress Control Number: 2024900891

First Edition: January 2024
Edited by Amanda Ordaz, Lauren Chavez, and Velia LaGarda
Published by Word Paddle, 27315 Parklane Way, Valencia, CA, USA
www.wordpaddle.com

Your Ears Aren't THAT Big

To Gabby, Amanda and Adam
You inspire me.

CONTENTS

RUNNING THROUGH SPRINKLERS

INTRODUCTION

Meditation is a practice that I aspire to master someday. I think it would enhance my life in many ways. Imagine leaving behind your physical body and observing the world from a higher perspective. I would cultivate a deep appreciation for life, love, connection and service. My passion to make a positive difference in the world would intensify. The challenge is, I always doze off whenever I attempt to meditate. I have never been good at following directions. So, for now, I am content with watching things from ground level. I enjoy being a passenger in a car, cruising along with the rest of you, admiring the scenery and listening to the sounds of the road. But this passenger also likes to jot down her thoughts.

These thoughts have turned into a book. Well, not exactly a book. It's more like a compilation of ideas, insights and nuggets of wisdom. Think of it as pieces of macadamia nuts on a giant cookie. It's so informal that I actually finished putting it together while hanging out with my daughter Amanda and friend Emily at urgent care.

During a three-hour wait in urgent care, I persuaded and fooled Amanda into helping me shape this "book". In reality, all the people mentioned in this book helped shape my view of life. Family, friends and total strangers have given me a strong understanding of life and its dwellers. Main characters in this booklet of life are my three kids. Amanda is my middle one. Gabby is the eldest. Adam is the youngest. All in their 20s during this compilation.

Anyway, I am telling you all this because I want you to relax and enjoy this booklet. Choose and read a topic that appeals or pulls at you on any given day. And if you get a laugh or a glimpse of enlightenment, maybe you can share some bits in conversation with other passengers. Many of the topics are relatable, quirky, mostly unscientific, and constantly laced with a ribbon of self-mockery. I am not a therapist, but I pretend to be one on TV (hehe). Seriously, I am neither a spiritualist nor a life coach. I just show up to the game…always ready to bat. Dodging and catching. I asked my kids to pick a favorite piece of writing. Amanda likes "Baggage Claim of Thoughts". Gabby prefers the one about her, "He Loves me, He Love me Not?" Adam says "Foil Paper in Microwave" is funky. So, make sure you read those. Also, look at the back of this book. There, you'll find a picture of me. You will see that my ears are actually not THAT big.

YOUR EARS AREN'T THAT BIG

IT ALL DEPENDS ON HOW YOU LOOK AT THINGS

PART 1

YOUR EARS
AREN'T THAT BIG

≈

During my college years, I worked at a grocery store with one of my best friends, Athena. One day, Athena noticed that I was feeling down. She inquired, "What's wrong Rosa, you seem sad?" I bemoaned, "Well, I have a big nose, big ears, dark circles under my eyes, big lips, long toes and frizzy hair." Athena tenderly placed her hand on my shoulder and said, "Awwh, don't be so down on yourself Rosa, your ears aren't that big." I laugh every time I remember this.

Athena was right, my ears aren't that big. And if they are, that just makes me a better listener.

I don't have a problem pointing out or even laughing at my physical imperfections. In fact, during middle school, I would joke with inner-circle friends about the size of my nose. I even allowed them to call me *Nosa*, instead of Rosa. With an air of confidence, I would often clarify, *It's not that my nose is big, it's just that my face is small.*

Our body and face are shells that encapsulate our physicality. But what dances inside the shell is what matters most. The way we perceive both outer and inner is what takes center stage. Our mindset

5

can galvanize or deflate our spirit. So, it is important to have constant conversations with perception. Sometimes things are not as bad as they appear.

BAGGAGE CLAIM
OF THOUGHTS

When breakups and stuff
get stuck on the conveyor belt

≈

One of my nieces recently experienced a break-up. After one year, her boyfriend broke up with her by text. The breakup was abrupt and unexpected. Similarly, after ten years of loyal work, one of my good friends was recently fired from her job. Unforeseen termination of a relationship, whether personal or professional, can leave one floating in disbelief. It can feel like someone pulled the rug from under you, like you're slipping on banana peels. You are floored! You have suffered an attack on the heart and mind.

We have all heard, *time will help heal your heart.* Oftentimes, the driver of the healing process is your mind. But what if your mind is clogged with circulating thoughts? What can help ease your mind? My immediate advice to my niece is this: get rid of the baggage and turbulence in your mind.

Picture yourself at an airport. After you deplane, one suitcase awaits you at the baggage claim. You walk through the airport carrying an overstuffed-aging carry-on bag. When you make it to Baggage Claim 3, you rush over to collect your suitcase. You're alone when you spot your suitcase as it is being spit out at the mouth of the conveyor belt. As you get closer, a dozen suitcases drop onto the conveyor belt. You pick up your suitcase, and soon you start picking up other suitcases. Before long, your arms are overwhelmed by half a dozen suitcases. You cannot carry them all. The situation is unmanageable.

Similarly, trying to manage a marching band of thoughts is unsustainable. My advice to my niece continued. Each night, as you're going to bed, as a chain of thoughts awaits your mind, make a decision to only manage one suitcase. Only pick up the suitcase that holds your essentials for the next day. Only choose the suitcase that can help move the needle forward, not backward. All the other suitcases (thoughts) will weigh you down; equally, watching these suitcases (thoughts) circle around your mind, will prove fruitless.

What did I do wrong? Why didn't I see this coming? What will I do next? My future was tethered to this relationship. Was I not good enough? How can people be so cold-hearted? I need closure.

You need to leave those thoughts on the runway. Yes, you will be left yearning for closure. But know that closure comes at its own pace and in its own fashion.

In that one shiny suitcase, decide to carry only your roadmap for the next day; when you're able to manage more, glance ahead at next week. Before you know it, that suitcase will have unfurled all the clothing you need for one month. As months scale the calendar, you will find that one suitcase is all you need. And, in terms of that overstuffed-aging carry-on bag, life's boarding pass will let you know when it's time for a new one.

ROSES ARE RED,
VIOLETS ARE BOLD

≈

It's been said that not all that glitters is gold. I would add that not all that is subdued is bland. Sometimes the blaze is within.

A rainbow produces different colors, each emitting varying levels of energy. I was surprised to learn that when measured, the color red actually contains less energy than some of its partners on the spectrum. Just like the colors of a rainbow, we all come in different hues and spike different levels of energy and personalities. Just as the color of a rainbow, the vibrancy that radiates inside each individual may not be reflected on the outside. We are unique and mysterious.

While on the outside a person may seem dim in appearance, there could be vibrancy, strength and a firm sense of self on the inside. So, we should not underestimate the timid colors. For example, Violet. In reading about color psychology, I learned that according to old Chakra beliefs, violet purifies our thoughts and feelings, giving us inspiration in all undertakings. The violet energy connects us to our spiritual self, bringing guidance, wisdom and inner strength. The color enhances artistic talent and creativity.

I also learned that the rainbow color that radiates the most energy is, indeed, Violet. Red waves have a relatively long wavelength (700 nm range). Violet waves have a much shorter wavelength, about half of that. Because violet waves have the shortest wavelength of the visible light spectrum, they carry the most energy.

We can apply the rainbow model to the people realm. For example, let's take job status or title. Some wear suit-and-tie and sit in the big office, while others push mops and clean toilets in office buildings. That same custodian may have a home that's rich in love and laughter, while the suit could go home to a rigid welcome or vice-versa. We are not all privy to the wavelengths inside others. Simply observing a person's exterior doesn't tell the whole story of who they are. Some of us are violets, reds, blues or yellows.

There's a formula to remember the colors and the order of the rainbows. It's: ROY G. BIV. Red, orange, yellow green, blue, indigo and violet. You see, although violet finishes last, it's actually the strongest. Strength is measured from within. Sometimes rainbows save the best for last.

ARE YOU A MOUNTAIN OR AN OLD GOAT?

It all depends on how you look at things

≈

An old friend, Joey, and I went hiking near the beach one summer. We didn't find the hike too challenging; so, instead of following the established path closer to the water, we decided to trek the side of a hill. As we reached the walking path, two ladies neared us. One joked, "I saw you two coming down that big hill. Boy, you guys are like 'mountain goats'!" After we passed the women, Joey turned and whispered, "Did you hear that? She called me an old goat!" To which I replied, "Did you hear that? She called me a mountain!"

It all depends on how you look at things.

One of my best friends (let's call her Camille) met financial hurdles recently. Camille is an amazing artist. She can also play the piano, sell houses, cut hair, sew clothes; and she happens to be one of my favorite cooks. Camille even owned a restaurant at one point. Due to the unexpected, my friend has started working as a caregiver for an older, sick person. The work of a caregiver can be physically and emotionally challenging. Camille tells me that sometimes, if all goes well, it can take up to an hour and a half to assist her patient in using the restroom. Camille is petite, but strong and determined. In addition to caring for her client, she helps around their house and cooks some pretty delicious meals. Her patient and his wife appear to be quite content with Camille's work. It aches me, though, to picture my friend struggling so hard to make a living. I suggested to Camille, *maybe you should look for something less strenuous and stressful.*

Camille quickly negated my concern, saying, "I don't look at this job as something bad. I look at it as if I'm getting paid to go to school. I'm learning how to take care of someone. Yes, this is a tough case. But as I learn more and more, I can take my experience to another job. Down the line, I can choose my clients and more conducive arrangements. Plus, I'm helping out another human being. So, you see, I'm lucky." She smiled and we moved on to another topic.

I reflected on Camille's positive perspective. I wondered about the source of her strength, wisdom and sunniness. Does this come from her mind, her spirituality, or her heart? Maybe it comes from all three.

Camille's take on things serves as a reminder that we have a choice in how we look at struggles, hardships, or how we see ourselves amidst an ocean of challenges. This takes me back to a rosy quote from Abraham Lincoln:

"We can complain because rose bushes have thorns, or rejoice because thorn bushes have roses."

Will you center your eyes on the petals and smell the roses this week? Or will you focus on gripping the thorns?

Not long after my conversation with Camille, I heard a *Beatles* song, "Hey Jude" (McCartney, 1973). Singing it, Paul McCartney nudges us to take a sad song and make it better. Yes, let's make it better!

IF IT WALKS LIKE A DUCK…

≈

When in grammar school, I walked like a duck. I forget who pointed this out to me. Regardless, it was then that I decided to straighten my walk. It may have taken months or years, but my duck walk had eventually subsided. Shockingly, now decades later, the duck walk has returned.

While walking our dog in our new neighborhood recently, my husband shot a minute of video to send our kids. I asked to see the video, before sending. My head snapped. *What the heck! Who is that person, and why is she walking like a duck? Did you notice this?* My husband politely tilted his head, "Well, I have noticed a little, but…"

How can you not tell me I've been walking like a duck this whole time?

Ugh! My feet and legs were reverting to their childhood ways. And it was all caught on video! Although my duck walk is more subtle now, I still see shades of the familiar legs-apart and feet-turned-outward.

Many of us nestle efforts to change our walk, straighten our backs or tuck in our stomachs. However, sometimes there are forces that work against these endeavors. For example, I know a young lady who works remotely. After hitting the snooze button once or twice in the morning, Sam rolls over and sits up in bed. Her pillows provide limited support; she spends several hours slightly hunched over her laptop. It is likely that, down the line, Sam will have to make a cognizant effort to align her posture.

As we move through life, we might notice things that need a little bit of pruning or tucking. So, we do the snipping and make the adjustments. However, sometimes new feats provoke us, and our attention strays away from the now "has-been" problems. We find ourselves relaxing on particular fronts. Our bones return to their familiar sockets. We become less worried about this, and more worried about the new blemish.

Since my elementary school days so much has come up on my "need to adjust" radar. So, I have accommodated. Eyeglasses improve my vision; braces straighten my teeth; hair color covers…well you get my point. Admittingly, there is one area I have never addressed…my dance moves. Folks it never ends! I can make a duck-umentary about all this.

Circling back to my duck walk. After some reflection on my regression to the pond, I have decided not to sweat it. I will simply adjust when I notice a significant divergence in the way I paddle.

At the start of each new year, some of us resolve to make changes that will adjust and improve some parts of ourselves. Eventually, some of our resolutions for change can meander a little. I suggest that we should not be so hard on ourselves when this happens. Taking such a posture will not make you a lame duck, truly.

Not everything has to be perfect. Take a lesson from the book, *Henry's Awful Mistake,* written by Robert M. Quackenbush. This book is about a Duck who is trying to cook a nice meal for his friend Clara. While he is cooking, he sees an ant and tries to kill it. He keeps missing and ends up destroying everything in the process of trying to kill a tiny ant.

Don't let the tiny ants destroy your duck soup.

*A quick disclaimer. I have read that in some cases, one's duck walk may have more to do with the way one's hips are aligned. Although the feet do not look aligned or neutral, the hip joint will likely be just that, neutral, sitting nicely in the hip joint/socket.

DEFLECTING BIG LIPS

≈

When I was in middle school, a group of us students took a field trip to the snow. For some, it was their first time touching snow. After a full day of snowball tossing, sledding and other hearty snow play, we made it back onto the bus. We were exhausted.

I ended up sitting next to one of my best friends' younger brother, Billy. I suspected Billy had a crush on me, but I didn't really give it much mind. Within minutes of the drive back down the mountain, I fell into a heavy sleep. At one point, I opened my eyes and found Billy intently looking at my face. Half asleep, I tilted my head as I studied the situation. Suddenly, out of nowhere, Billy exclaimed, "Man, you've got some big lips!" And that was the launching point of my nickname. I would be known as "Lips" through the remainder of my middle school life. I didn't mind, most of the time. I typically only grudged when my peers called me Lips in a classroom setting, when teachers were around. My teachers sometimes smirked and other times paused, as if wondering something.

This big avalanche of my middle school nickname was triggered by Billy deflecting his feelings for me. He obviously had a crush on me. He had watched me as

I slept in the bus, and when I woke to find him in la-la land, he hid his embarrassment by deflecting. He criticized my looks, specifically one of my prominent features, so that I wouldn't suspect he liked me.

Many of us have been Billy's at one point or another. We deflect. We may be conscious of it, as I suspect Billy was. I suspect that politicians are also aware when they deflect from challenging reporter questions. At times, some of us may have only an inkling of something odd brewing. I recall a time when I was interviewed for a job. I was asked if my skill set included knowledge of Adobe Illustrator. *What?* I answered by starting off with the many other skillsets that I do master. But at the end of my long-winded answer, I did admit to having distant knowledge of the graphics design program.

Deflecting can happen in different settings, like in the workplace or in personal relationships. There are pitfalls to deflecting in the workplace. Betterhelp.com posted an article on the pitfalls of deflection. The article gives an example of an employee, Jamie, who heads a work project. When Jamie makes a significant error, he's called into the boss' office. Instead of admitting to the mistake, Jamie deflects. He's unwilling to accept failure, so he shifts the blame on another co-worker or on management. His deflecting, and inability to take ownership, diminishes Jamie's credibility.

There is a domino effect to deflecting. You reroute the conversation down a different path. This can have minimal or long-lasting ramifications. In the case of Billy shouting to the world that I had big lips, well, I had to live with that nickname for a couple years. But what about the small white lies that just help you through your day? Take my son Adam for example. When he was in high school, preparing for college, I asked if he had filled out any scholarship applications to help ease the financial burden. Adam replied, "Yes, I looked at a couple and read through some of the prompts." Essentially, no, Adam had not filled out any scholarship applications. But instead of admitting, or lying about it, he told a truth that for the time being helped him deflect.

People can lie by telling the truth. The American Psychological Association recognized the pervasiveness of this practice; back in 2016, the association gave it a name, *paltering*. According to APA, "Paltering is the active use of truthful statements to convey a misleading impression."

So basically, when Billy said I have big lips, he was telling a truth.

BIG TEETH IN FRONT, LITTLE TEETH IN BACK

≈

While biting into an avocado toast one summer, I chipped a tooth. Actually, I chipped a veneer that covered a compromised tooth. I couldn't dial my dentist fast enough! After a quick temporary fix at the neighborhood dentist, I visited my original dentist for a deep cleaning and repair work. I had not seen this particular dentist in a while, and I noticed a few new faces in the room. One of them was the hygienist, who was assigned to do a deep dive into my mouth. Let's call him Roger. Somehow, Roger also managed to floss my mind a little.

Roger had a monotone demeanor in more ways than one. He spoke the entire time. And each time that he needled me with Novocaine, Roger's stories got wilder. Maybe his plan was to distract me. Roger talked about the many different individuals whom he helped heal - special needs adults, prisoners, musicians, actors and the elderly (some who carried the label DNR, do not resuscitate). Roger buttoned up his observations a couple of times by stating, "At the end of the day, we're all the same. Big teeth in the front, little teeth in the back."

No one's perspective has intrigued me as much as Roger's. Curious, I opened my eyes a few times, trying to size him up. But his face covering only exposed his eyes. I did notice some creases on his neck. By contrast, Roger could see my whole face and the most humiliating part of myself - an embarrassing chipped tooth! Roger had no problem sizing me up, "I can't read minds, but I can read faces. What I see is that the dentist is not your thing, and you're a busy woman." I guess that means: *lady you don't make time for your teeth.* Ugh! But I floss ALL the time!

Roger also said a couple of things that evoked chuckles and groans, or whatever sound I could muster. In a wondering-type voice, Roger said, "People leave here faster than they come in, I don't know why? Sometimes people get mad or annoyed with me, because of their mouths. I tell them, *why are you mad at me? I don't even know you. It's your mouth. You're the one who's done that.*"

I agree with Roger's precise observation about our teeth. From his vantage point, Roger's lenses don't get fogged up with people's titles, bank accounts, trophies, salaries, estates, bells and whistles. Roger sees the rawness of all humans. It's as if he gets to see our skeletons. From that perspective, I'm sure the core of us seems pretty similar.

So, here are several lessons (gifts) I got from that last dental visit:

- Don't think others are better than you; and don't think yourself better than others.

- Hold yourself accountable for the way you treat your body, mind and teeth.
- Visit Roger more often.

HIGH HEELS
AND RENTAL CARS

≈

I avoid wearing high heels as much as possible. My toes just don't like that tight, claustrophobic feeling or the downward slope. This is why, in a professional setting, I often wear pants that blend well with a pair of comfortable yet sturdy shoes.

One autumn day, I gave a tour to some visitors at my workplace, so I wore a dress and high heels for the occasion. Miserably, my feet were throbbing by the end of the day. So as soon as I made it to my car, I kicked off my heels. After a one-hour commute home, I pulled into my driveway, which provided dim lighting. I searched around for my shoes under the car seat, and put them back on my feet.

As I made my way to the front door and then into the house, my feet were ready to burst from the squeeze of my shoes. It was as if either my shoes had shrunk, or as if my feet had mega swelled. The displeasure was acute! After turning on a couple of lights and making my way to the bedroom, I realized that my shoes were each on the wrong foot. Yikes! Right foot in left shoe, left foot in right shoe. I corrected the situation and sighed in relief. Aaah, the shoes felt so much better. I gazed at my feet sink into the shoes for a few seconds, before taking them off. The shoe mishap reminded me that things can always be worse. The throbbing I had experienced while walking around my office building was nothing in comparison to the chokehold my feet suffered under the later shoe mishap.

Things can always be worse.

Midweek, the check engine light went on in my car. I took it back to the mechanic, who had serviced my car days earlier. While I waited in the lobby, I overheard a customer dropping off a car, and asking the employee at the counter, "Can someone give me a ride to Enterprise Rent A Car?" The employee said no, but that he could call Enterprise. The customer (let's call him Ron) explained that he had already called Enterprise, but that Enterprise would not be able to get him for some time; Ron did not want to be late for work. The employee suggested to Ron that he ask his tow truck driver for a lift. Enterprise was just over one mile away. The tow truck driver said, "No bud, can't, sorry, I gotta run." By now, my check engine light issue was fixed. An employee drove my car to the front door. I turned to Ron and said, "I can give you a ride." Ron and the employees were relieved. I'm a regular customer, so the workers trust me. Ron grabbed his gadgets and hopped into my car.

On our drive, I told Ron that I had overheard him explaining that someone had hit his car and caused mechanical problems. Ron's other car was also at another auto repair place. I lamented to Ron, "Man, that's too bad. It's always something, right? If it's not one thing, it's another." Ron turned his head slightly in my direction and affirmed, "I'm actually a lot better today than at any point in my life."

Ron's face appeared serious, stern, stressed, but with a hint of determination. I nodded in agreement, "Wow, I guess it's all about perspective. It's how we look at things."

The drive was 1.4 miles and lasted likely four minutes. But the lesson came in a one sentence message. *I'm actually a lot better today than at any point in my life.*

As I ponder that statement, I am respectfully aware that for some, right now, marks one of the worse points in their lives. This, especially if one has experienced a shocking loss, or has been at the receiving end of nature's rath, like a deadly wildfire or an earthquake.

While uncomfortable high heels and car problems can annoy or rattle us, we are often aware of the fixes. Although we cannot readily fix the broken hearts of others, experiencing grief, or unimaginable tragedy, we can all pitch in to make a tiny difference in the lives of those we can help. Why not offer a simple (safe) ride to a neighbor, or a warm meal to a friend? We can use our available lanterns to lend light to the cracks in the rubble.

WHEN DOGGIE NAMES ENTER DANGER ZONE

≈

Before our dog Jango came into our lives, back in 2013, my kids and I visited a dog pound in search of our first family dog. Inside the animal shelter, I noticed that most of the cages were labeled with dog names. Reading the labels was fun; it seemed to me that the assigned names somehow matched the doggies' vibes. I wondered where the workers got their inspirations. Even some human names, like Stan, seemed to be quirky matches.

Near the end of our visit, we walked through an area that was slightly detached from the rest of the facility. Upon entering, I took notice of a dog that seemed a little hostile. Although this Pit Bull did not cozy up, I maintained a friendly demeanor. Ignoring his growing growling and barking, I blissfully turned to my kids, "Oh how cute, his name is *Peligro*. Wow! And his name is in such big letters!" I then noticed another sign: 'Beware'.

Oops, I knew the Spanish word Peligro translates to Danger. It took me a minute to figure out that I was in the "dangerous dogs" zone.

At times, we may see what we want to see, or we see what we think we are supposed to see. Eventually, life's signals come into play and help sort things out, pointing out the green lights and the STOPs. Ultimately, it's on us to read the signs and discern the situations. Some of us who have stumbled or misread a sign might kick ourselves, "Wow, how could I have been so silly? Why didn't I see that huge, red flag?" But I reason that part of gaining growth and wisdom requires navigating through some blind spots.

Perhaps those moments of naïve inclinations provide a respite for our minds and allow us to consider varying possibilities or perspectives. Or, could a temporary adjournment be a little recess our mind needs, in order to survive life's realities? Yes, willful blindness can be a funky cane.

The dog incident was not the first time that I misread a situation. Perhaps I allow my mind to wonder a little bit more than the average person. I notice that I am often intentionally alert to situations that might require assistance. Part of me is always on the lookout for opportunities to help. Take an incident involving the bus ladies.

Late summer, dipping off the evening commute, I exited the 5 Freeway in Los Angeles and drove home on a busy stretch of highway. I took notice of two Latina ladies running with intention. One of them reminded me of my aunt in Mexico. Seeing their pace pick up, I worried, presuming they were trying to catch a bus. *They probably got off work late and are gonna miss their bus,* I thought. I wondered if I should make a right at the next street, turn around and offer them a ride; this, if they had indeed missed their bus. As I continued south, I kept a keen eye for the bus stop. *Hmm, that's strange*. I didn't see a bus stop on that particular stretch of road. I looked back toward the ladies and noticed the two were dressed similarly. They were each wearing dark jogging suits. Aaah! They were not running to catch a bus; they were simply jogging to exercise. Being Latina myself, I had grown up knowing many hard-working men and women whose only means of transportation was the bus. This time though, I presumed incorrectly. Shame on me. My personal bias had me overcompensating, needlessly.

So, note to self: pay closer attention to signals and signs.

Second note to self: don't lose your silly naivety or willingness to help. And keep remembering that not all Pit Bulls are dangerous.

ROADBLOCKS AND CURVEBALLS

≈

My son Adam was headed back to Cal Poly San Luis Obispo for a summer 2023 research project. Despite my suggestion to take a straight road back along the California coast, Adam and his girlfriend opted to drive on a winding mountain road. Concerned because he drives an older car, and because his car once got stuck on a bridge, I asked Adam to keep me posted on his drive. I'm glad I did.

Last time, when Adam got stuck on a bridge, he was driving home from his girlfriend's place. Adam opted to take the shorter route, but this road was also darker and curvy. Unfortunately, along the way, a large delivery truck somehow partially tilted and snarled the two-lane bridge. The worst part of this was that Adam had no cell service. Needless to say, I did not sleep that night. Finally, around 4 a.m., a nervous and shaky Adam was able to call me. He apologized emphatically for causing the family to worry.

We both learned from that experience. This time around, I made sure to track his location on my phone. I was relieved to see that Adam had stopped at a hamburger place along the coast, located 30 minutes from his final destination. Sigh. They were almost home. Surprisingly, just as I snuggled back onto my pillow at 11:30 p.m., my phone beeped, "Mom, we're stuck, there's a roadblock. We're ten minutes away, but we're not moving."

I logged onto a CHP site, which reported a multi-vehicle collision at Adam's location. Adam was right, traffic was not moving in either direction. Thankfully, after about an hour, part of the road cleared, and Adam was on his way. I went back to sleep after the last message, "We are home!"

I found it ironic that so much of my worry was placed on the winding mountainous road, when the actual roadblock was on a straight highway, ten minutes from home. This just goes to show that while we are often able to negotiate life's curves, our navigation can get tossed a curveball.

Sometimes the obstacles in life seem pretty obvious. Other times, obstacles pop up from unsuspecting places. Detours can include things like a blocked job or promotion, a break in a romantic relationship or the losing of a sports championship. One cannot always avoid life's detours, but the best one can do is be prepared.

When Adam got stuck on the bridge, he was equipped with some essentials: phone and charger, water, food and a tracking system. Adam had also packed his tablet, which had plenty of battery life to play a saved movie. This certainly helped.

We don't always know the items we will need to pull out from our emergency kit. However, we can pack the best attitudes for any situation: mental clarity, discernment, diplomacy, positivity, resourcefulness, and determination.

Just Spray
and Walk Away

≈

The instructions on the bottle read, "Just spray and walk away". Done! I tossed the bathroom cleaner into my shopping cart. Mildew had been building up in my shower, and this product seemed like the perfect solution. I got home, sprayed, and walked away. Hours later, I checked in on my shower. Hmm, not much had changed. Begrudgingly, I grabbed a sponge and scrubbed. Hmm, the mildew remained stubborn. Why does the world lie to me?

There are a handful of cleaning products for bathrooms that in the past have indeed allowed me to simply spray and walk away. Wouldn't it be something if when dealing with life's sticky problems we could simply spray a quick-fix and walk away? But for me, this time around, the product was not a match; the operation required a sponge and my participation...some elbow grease. This serves as a reminder that sometimes dealing with situations is not always easy. Sometimes, certain situations require different products or approaches.

Now, diverging to a different kind of spray, hairspray. We girls (and guys) have tried varying brands and *holds*: light hold, medium hold, mega hold. It takes a few trial-and-errors to find the perfect hold for our hair type. The importance of the right hairspray cannot be overrated. Oftentimes, it's the last touchup, with which we drizzle ourselves before heading out the door.

Crockpots can also provide that walk-away option. Admittingly, I am not the best cook. Typically, I prefer managing only 3-step recipes. Crockpots can be a good option for people like me. I like the convenience they offer; drop a piece of meat into the crockpot, sprinkle salt and pepper or other seasonings, and walk away.

I googled for more benefits of using a crockpot and found the following: gradual cooking enhances flavors, meat becomes tender, you won't burn your food, and your meals will be healthier.

I found an old poem which I penned many years ago, and it's titled 'Crockpot of the Soul'. The poem was riddled with varied descriptors: gasping for air, drowning in humanness, undercurrents of the beautiful abyss, anxiety, uncertainty, and inability to process current stress. Although the poem doesn't sound very uplifting, it does remind me that we too can be like tiny crockpots, that collaborate with the chef (the soul), allowing our individuality, experiences and states of mind to simmer in tenderness.

I wonder whether, subconsciously, we knowingly drop all of our complexities into an internal crockpot and allow our soul to do the elbow-greasing.

You look
just like your father...

Your father was an ugly man

≈

Perhaps it was a specific feature on my face that triggered my grandmother. Turning away from me and eyeing the distance, my loving grandma uttered, "You look just like your father. Your father was a very ugly man."

I am not sure exactly how seven-year-old me reacted to my late grandmother's observation. But it formed a memory in me that has scratched at me for years. Actually, it's more of a tickle than a scratch. I chuckle, because I know exactly what she meant. Like my grandmother, I too was aware of my estranged father's cruel treatment of my mother. Yes, he was ugly on the inside. Although, I find it funny that my *Nana* was so immersed in her thoughts that she didn't take into account this child's sensibilities.

Allow me to lean into this memory on two separate tracks.

For one, perhaps my grandmother should have read the room before reading her thoughts out loud. Afterall, I was a young girl barely forming my identity and self-perception. But, even if I had been older and coated with thicker skin, my ears would have heard the same thing. So, to the Nanas in all of us: Yes, your thoughts and opinions matter, but consider who is in the room to catch the apples that you toss into the air.

Taking an alternative view at that moment, that little girl (me) was pretty much being told that her father was no looker, and neither was she. How did this little girl not hide under a pillow and drown in self-sorrow? The answer, my dear readers, is in this book. I can tease myself and my outer shell, with little hesitation. Self-deprecation? Yes, I have big lips, big nose, and kind of big ears, et cetera. I can do this, because I actually have a strong sense of self…my inner self. I was lucky enough to grasp that postulation early on. While I was not born a princess or a queen, I sometimes walk around with an invisible crown. And while that crown can tilt a little (as alluded to by a Rumi poem, *When Our Crowns Go Crooked*), my strides maintain a steadiness.

I choose to write uplifting messages as a way of reminding you, the reader, that you too have access to this invisible crown. Pack it in your bag and take it everywhere you go. This way, whenever someone utters a negative thought at your expense, you won't necessarily need the shield of thick skin. You can simply bring out your elegant crown and gracefully polish it.

SCALES AND MIRRORS

≈

Whenever I take my dog Jango to the vet, he resists getting on the scale. Jango is half Labrador, half German Shephard. While he's big-boned, I don't think Jango is hung up on his weight; he's just apprehensive in new environments. When I visit my doctor for a checkup, I am also uneasy about getting on the scale. I make it a point to wear light shoes, and I definitely remove my jacket and purse. Ultimately, I dismiss the final numbers on the scale, reminding myself that scales vary anyway. *They are never exact. Sometimes the time of day can also make a difference.* Scales vary in what they reflect back to us, just as mirrors do.

For my daughter's nineteenth birthday, I printed a photo of a chess pawn, looking in the mirror and seeing its true nature reflect back. The mirror exposes an image of a Queen on the other side. I wanted Amanda to see what I saw in her: beauty of the royal kind.

Just as with many of us, Amanda's self-esteem can dim at times. When that happens, I dive into action, ready to uplift her. However, after pondering about my well-intended mirror photo gift, I decided to steer my counsel in an opposite direction. I resolved to encourage Amanda to spend less time in front of mirrors. Yes, it's okay to check ourselves before we go out into the world. Perhaps we can consider that our time, and self-intake, is better spent reflecting on what echoes out from inside. Afterall, mirrors aren't always accurate, and they don't measure the aesthetics inside of us. Glossyfied.com tells us that lighting, warping, and glass thickness can cause you to look different in different mirrors. Apparently, clothing stores stack things in their favor by stocking their dressing rooms with skinny mirrors. If one sees a slimmer version of themselves in the store mirror, they are more likely to make a purchase. *Funny, dressing room mirrors always make me feel worse.* Regardless, my point is: What you see is not always what is.

In the book, 'Atomic Habits', author James Clear shares different formulas for success. When he talks about achieving weight loss goals, Clear discusses scales. He says that when we stand on a scale, we may initially feel discouraged by what we see. Clear advises that we be patient and not focus solely on the scale. He encourages readers to look at the other small victories that we gain along the way. For example, he says, you might notice that exercise and nutritional changes have netted other mini wins. You might notice better skin, or more energy in the mornings. Best not to put all your "weight" on what the scale reads back to you.

And just like scales and mirrors vary in what they read back to us; photographs also diverge. When someone takes a photo of me, for example, I ask that we take multiple photos, especially if the pics are for a post on social media. I like browsing the options and selecting the photo that is more complimentary. Some pics make us look slimmer or younger.

Perhaps scales, mirrors and quick pics only tell a partial story, and a truer measure is one's essence. As well told by essayist and poet Kahlil Gibran, "Beauty is not in the face; beauty is a light in the heart".

***

HE LOVES ME,
HE LOVES ME NOT...

LOVE YOURSELF

PART 2

HE LOVES ME,
HE LOVES ME...NOT?

≈

On a summer afternoon, my daughter Gabby called for boyfriend advice. "Mom, last week he told me he loves me, but he hasn't said it since." She wondered, *did he really mean it, or did he change his mind?* I reminded her that they had only been together four months. I suggested that she be patient with both of their emotions.

Well, Gabby is not good at sitting on her emotions. So, she discussed her trepidation with said boyfriend. He explained that he does care but acknowledged that their relationship is still in its infancy, and perhaps the words will hold truer in time. Gabby pouted, "Well, I think I'm pretty awesome. If he doesn't love me, then why should I invest more time?" In a passive-aggressive manner, Gabby told her boyfriend that she is not sure about the direction of their relationship. She cited *this-and-that*.

I suggested, "Don't focus on the words; look at his actions. How does he treat you? And if the words accidentally slipped from his mouth, it's because he does love you - as a special person in his life. Give it time." Unsatisfied, Gabby grumbled, "I just want someone to be obsessed with me." I know Gabby was thinking back to advice received from her aunt Blanca, "In a relationship, you don't want to be the hunter, you want them to hunt you."

I laughed and asked Gabby, "Do you think I'm awesome? Yes? Well, **I am** obsessed with you. So there, you have one awesome person obsessed with you. And I am sure your dad, brother and sister are obsessed with you too. Look, you have four people in the front row, looking up at you on stage. You don't need more than that. You don't need a man to be obsessed with you."

When Gabby calls with a problem, I first like to reassure her. Still, I always like to broaden her lens so that she can see the world around her, instead of just a world in which she is drowning, gasping for air.

A friend, Irene, posted a quote by motivating author Charlie Wardle. The words resonated: "A bird sitting on a tree is never afraid of the branch breaking, because her trust is not on the branch but on her own wings. Believe in yourself." This is a reminder to not hold others accountable for our happiness.

It feels great to be wanted, desired, and "adored" by others. However, if that romance branch breaks beneath us, we need to be able to rely on our own wings. If a special person in your life tells you they love you, and they stick around to nurture that love, excellent. But why not celebrate the love you have for yourself and rely on the power of your wings? The force to fly comes from within.

We can embolden those wings with the energy we bring into our lungs. The air we draw from giving, caring, and loving others is mighty. Life is not about waiting for a person to tell us that they love us, romantically. Life is about constantly planting and harvesting love from within, and then sharing the seeds of love with the world. Sometimes expressing our love for others – whether romantic or not – makes a difference.

Yes, it feels good to hear *those three words*. They are a reflection of the great things our partner sees in us; they are an affirmation. An article, in Psychology Today, points out that one of the things we forget to do is to tell ourselves that we are loved. Therefore, we tend to take the easy route and let others tell us.

So, my advice to Gabby is to grow in self-love and to spread love. Love comes back in many forms. *When you are expressing love to the important people in your life, you are also expressing it to yourself.* So instead of Gabby waiting for her boyfriend or other people to say, "I love you," she should make a conscious effort to say the words to herself, and to others. Love branches out.

EATING ROCKS

≈

Do you ever get that sick feeling in your stomach? It's a common experience, isn't it? You feel nauseous, nervous, or like your stomach is dropping. It could happen before a big exam, a job interview, or during a painful breakup. You feel sick to your stomach, as if a brick has taken residency in your gut. Now, can you imagine anyone intentionally wanting to experience the feeling of a brick or stones at the pit of their stomach? This would not make sense, right? Consider the Crocodile. Yeap, crocodiles and alligators intentionally swallow stones.

I read in Science Magazine that crocodiles do it because the stones help basic digestion. Rocks in a crocodile's stomach help crush and grate food, which could include large bones and hard shells. A related study provides another explanation for the gator's stone-swallowing. The observation is that a belly full of rocks helps boost bottom time on dives. Science Magazine tells us that crocodiles and alligators spend most of their time in the water, stalking prey and escaping from predators. Anything they can do to maximize their time below the surface is an advantage. Scientists ran a study and found that when alligators swallowed the rocks, prior to a dive, increased their dive time by 88 percent, or by 35 minutes.

This got me thinking about the things that we humans stomach, like harsh foods, stress and viruses. Our other organs take in a lot as well. For example, the lungs take in bad air quality: smoke, fumes, dust. What about our most sensitive organ, the heart? The list is long, both physiologically and emotionally.

Do you know anyone with rocks in their heart? Perhaps you've known people, whom you would describe as having "a heart of stone." One can wonder, *what made them stone-hearted*? Maybe the protective rocks in their hearts help crush the pain and break down the daggers or flails of life. Perhaps the weight of the stones helps keep them hidden, beneath the surface. Maybe staying below the pain is the only way they can survive the surface of life.

There are plenty of things that clog up the heart. A person experiencing pain might not garner the strength to cut through, so they surrender to the rocks. Others fight through and break down the stones, while others might be left with a little debris. Some might choose to simply stay emotionally clogged; but before long, the stones could end up taking most of the real estate in the heart.

Alligators seem to have chosen the rocky road. You don't have to. Force yourself to come above the surface and find palpable tools that can help break down the pain, anger or sadness. Choose to be resourceful and spit out the rocks that life has flung and dropped into you.

THINKING
OUTSIDE THE CIRCLES

≈

Whenever I draw a circle,
I immediately want to step out of it.

-R. Buckminster Fuller

Many years ago, my then-optometrist shared a story about his daughter. He really got a kick out of his preschooler's nonconformist ways. We will call this little girl, Ellie.

He talked about the time he gave Ellie a box of crayons. Drawing a circle on paper, he suggested that Ellie color the inside of the circle. Ellie took a crayon and filled in the circle, but in all black. Perplexed, he drew another circle and encouraged Ellie to try assorted colors and to stay inside the perimeter this time. Mischievous and a bit stewed, Ellie took an eraser and erased the circle. She cleared the hedges, and colored freestyle. The colors danced haphazardly inside and outside the soon-forgotten circle.

Ellie's scuffle with circles came to mind the other day, while I browsed through a bookstore in the Arts

District in Downtown Los Angeles. A quote, on the cover of a tiny sketchbook, prompted a smirk. "Whenever I draw a circle, I immediately want to step out of it." The words came from architect, R. Buckminster Fuller.

Mr. Fuller's sentence stirred my senses. Invigorated, I wanted to jump outside myself and simply dance. Weird, right? I love coming across things that unlock a little bit of something from within. I dug a little into the architect's background and learned that Mr. Fuller was a 20th century inventor and visionary who did not limit himself to one field; but worked as a "comprehensive anticipatory design scientist to solve global problems". (https://www.bfi.org/)

I learned of Fuller's many accomplishments, which included twenty-five patents. However, I snickered a little when reading that Fuller entered Harvard University in 1913 but was expelled after excessively socializing and missing his midterm exams. He took a break from academics and worked with machinery, learning to modify and improve manufacturing equipment. Fuller returned to Harvard in 1915 but was again dismissed. *Sigh*, that nonconformist.

Of Fuller's many inventions, the one that dominated his life and career was the geodesic dome. Lightweight, cost-effective, and easy to assemble, geodesic domes that can withstand extremely harsh conditions.

In 1953, Fuller designed his first commercial dome for the Ford Motor Company headquarters in Dearborn, Michigan. The U.S. military became one of his biggest clients, using lightweight domes to cover radar stations at installations around the Arctic Circle.

I find it interesting that a man, who constantly placed himself outside the circle, created domes. Domes, as you know, resemble a hollow upper part of a sphere…not a full sphere. Just like Ellie, Fuller had entanglements with circles.

Now and then, I wonder what became of young Ellie; she must be in her early twenties. I picture her paving rocky roads. She is busy building rocket ships that crack the sound barrier. Wherever she is, I am almost certain Ellie spends a lot of time jumping and creating outside the circle.

In sharing my ruminations, I am not promoting unhealthy rebellion or law-breaking conduct. But just like that tiny quote stirred a little bit of spring in my spirit, I simply hope to rouse you to spring out, paint, color, dance, and splash yourself outside the circle. Do not just think outside the box, play outside the circle. Life is a playground that can fuel momentum and creativity.

In that spirit, I leave you with the words of Henry David Thoreau:

If a man does not keep pace with his companions, perhaps it is because he hears a different drummer. Let him step to the music which he hears, however measured or far away.

TAKE YOUR WORRIES
AND STUFF 'EM...IN A BOX

≈

Worry does not empty tomorrow of its sorrow.
It empties today of its strength.

-Corrie Ten Boom

Sometimes, worrying is for naught. My daughter, Amanda, is a worry bird. Even as a child, she worried about everything. Her disquiet got so bad that finally, one day, I asked Amanda to gather her worries and hand them over to me, literally. We engaged in this ritual countless times. My little girl would shyly hand over the invisible worries, and I would symbolically stuff them in my pants pocket. Each time we did this, Amanda seemed to feel better. Out of sight, out of mind.

Incessantly worrying about something might propel us into action, which could help dilute that particular worry. However, I have also observed that worrying can be counterproductive and could instead rob our minds of ideas and industrious inspirations. So, why give wings to worry? Why not store away relentless, caustic thoughts that could be stalling us?

To illustrate my point, I lean on a poem by Bertha Adams Backus. Here's a slice:

The Laugh
Build for yourself a strong box,
Fashion each part with care;
When it's strong as your hand can make it,
Put all your troubles there;
Hide there all thought of your failures,
And each bitter cup that you quaff;
Lock all your heartaches within it,
Then sit on the lid and laugh.

Several years ago, I experienced car problems. A friend introduced me to a fairly reasonable and inexpensive mechanic. This mechanic tuned up my car and got it road-ready fairly quickly. However, the mechanic also diagnosed a looming problem. My car's wheel bearings would need replacement in the future. Parts and labor would likely add up to about $700. With bills tugging at me each week, I could not schedule a follow-up visit to the mechanic. I worried about this constantly, wondering when I would have extra money for the repairs. I must have worried for several months. Then, one day, Amanda (yes, my worry bird) crashed my car, totaling it.

Thankfully, Amanda was not injured. While at a red light, she prematurely hit the gas pedal and rammed a Hummer in front. Our insurance covered everything, and I bought a different car. Turned out, all that worrying about my wheel bearings was for naught. By the way, this is not meant to encourage neglect of car maintenance. I hope this can serve as a reminder that life finds a way of tuning and pruning the road. We often don't know what's ahead. Sometimes, the unpredictable happens. Life is the eventual driver, managing the road.

So, if there's something that you need to address, either make a plan to remedy the situation, or choose not to worry about it. Yes, make a plan, worry less, and know that everything you're facing right now could reshape itself or be non-existent five years from now.

In recent articles, psychologist and writer, Nick Wignall, points out that worry gives you the illusion of certainty. *Worry is our attempt to out-run helplessness. And while it never works in the long run, we keep trying because it very briefly works in the short term, albeit with the unhappy side effect that we stay stressed and anxious in exchange for the illusion of control.* Wignall says that when you stop beating yourself up with all the stress and anxiety that comes with chronic worry, you'd be surprised how much energy and enthusiasm returns to your life.

If there is something on your mind, find a way to manage it. If a solution is out of your immediate control, then make a plan. If there is no viable strategy, wittingly place it inside your **Box of Worries**. It is when you get stuck in a cycle of repeated thoughts that you stall your walk. Why not rearrange the furniture in your mind? Pack that space with vivacity and build on the strength of ideas. Shift your focus. Do remember, though, that talking with someone about your worries can oftentimes provide relief, practical feedback, or even a pocket for storage.

I leave you with words from Camille Paglia:
We must accept our pain, change what we can, and laugh at the rest.

Shift your focus. Transform your thoughts. Embolden your mind.

THE VIOLINIST

≈

A man, holding a violin, sat a few feet from the grocery store entrance. Hoping to hear a little of his tunes, I slowed a bit before entering. At that moment, however, the man was simply moving the violin bow up and down, angling it a bit as if he was testing out the sounds before committing. I thought it would be awkward to simply drop money into his violin case, without first hearing him play. I didn't want to offend the musician with upfront charity. So, I decided to contribute money on my way out. By then, he would surely be playing a song. Perhaps.

After my shopping, I pulled a dollar from my wallet, getting it ready to drop it into the empty violin case (hmm, I could swear there was money in it earlier). But again, no song. The man appeared to be testing out his violin, with no consistent rhythm emanating. Slightly begrudged, I nevertheless dropped my committed dollar into the case. He thanked me…with exaggerated integrity.

Moments later, the violinist placed the dollar into his pocket and began loading up his belongings. As I loaded my car trunk with groceries, I noticed the man, with violin case in hand, make his way to a car. First,

I thought he was simply poking around the car. Perhaps he was being nosy or plotting a steal. I did a double take, as I watched him place his violin in the trunk. The car was not new, but also it was not a shabby BMW.

Did the man lie to me, or did I lie to myself?

That question brewed in me for a few days. Then, I stumbled on a quote that spun my thinking a little. Perhaps I was framing the man, his story, the violin, and myself prematurely.

The longer you silence a violin,
the harder it is for it to find its true voice again.
- Alexandra Bracken

WHEN YOU'RE DONE, YOU'RE DONE

≈

You've had enough! You're so over it! You're done! How does one know when they're really done with something or someone?

On a typical Sunday morning, and in typical Sunday frantic mode, I rushed out of the house and headed off to church with my young daughters, Gabby and Amanda. With no time for breakfast, I strapped on Gabby's seat belt and placed Amanda in a car seat. I handed them a couple of snacks and off we went. After church, as expected, the girls were hungry. We detoured to the nearest drive-thru before getting back onto the freeway. Gabby wanted her usual chicken nuggets and three-year-old Amanda opted for a hamburger. As I drove east on the 91 Freeway, traffic was moving at a good pace. Suddenly, out of nowhere, BOOM! Something hit the side of my head. I quickly looked around and found lettuce, bread and a portion of a beef patty scattered in the front seat of my car. An expressionless Amanda simply stated, "I'm done."

Many of us have likely observed a situation in which a person has expressed being done with something or someone. In Amanda's case, she was done with her burger and only knew to toss the leftovers in my direction.

After someone has endured an unpleasant situation or a perceived injustice, they might decide to simply walk away. One might walk out of a job, a marriage, a friendship or even a movie theater – like I did once when I watched 'No Country for Old Men.' I had incorrectly presumed the violence-ridden movie was about retirement. Anyway, back to the topic.

The late poet and activist Maya Angelou espoused, "If you don't like something, change it. If you can't change it, change your attitude." Being done means you have thought about a situation long enough, and you are ready to make a change. Change can be scary. This is likely why some people wait before deciding to cut a new path. Making a change can also connote that one is losing something that they once had. An article on psycom.net reminds us that change can also involve a sense of mourning. In the article, Kathleen Smith PhD, LPC tells us that even positive transitions – like a graduation or a job change – can make you feel a little sad. "During these times of transitions, don't push away any grief you might feel. Acknowledge the loss and pay attention to what you've learned from the experience."

When you acknowledge that you are done with something or someone, you are consciously transitioning to a new direction – you are choosing a different path. This can be empowering, as you are choosing something that brings you closer to your truth. You are choosing something that works for you. You are getting to know yourself better.

Smith's article also reminds us that the most resilient people see change as an opportunity rather than as a monster to fear. "Transitions in life allow you to consider where your priorities lie. How do you really want to spend your time on earth? What's really important to you?"

I have read several articles on the tugs of change. Most experts share similar advice, reminding us that in times of change it is important to pause, take deep breaths, lean into awareness and stay in the present.

When Amanda was done with her burger, she tossed the leftovers, stated her situation and remained in the present. If life could only be that simple.

WELL OF WEALTH

≈

Many of us spend a considerable amount of time buying the "right" clothes, choosing the best hairstyle, dieting and exercising. But while we busy ourselves with aesthetics, we might regrettably be placing more focus on our shortcomings, instead of on our natural, abundant shine. So, instead of trying to fix what's wrong with us, why not improve on our natural glitter?

Cleaning out my garage, I came upon some of my daughter's college textbooks. Amanda majored in psychology at Loyola Marymount University. LMU is a private and religious institution. So, Amanda dove deep into religion, philosophy and psychology. One of her textbooks proved to be a goldmine for me. And I hope you, the reader, can pull something from this as well.

The book, titled 'Strength Finder', is a great find indeed. It's actually more like cliff notes that take you to an on-line assessment test. The author encourages readers to figure out what's already right with them, and to embrace and harness their embedded talents.

The guide takes you through an exercise test to find out which of the 34 most common talents match you. Allow me to share just a slice of the book with you. For now, let's just simply look at its philosophy. Here's how the book starts:

"We (a group of scientists) were tired of living in a world that revolved around fixing our weaknesses. Society's relentless focus on people's shortcomings had turned into a global obsession." The author also points out something you may already know: *people have several times more potential for growth when they invest energy in developing their strengths instead of correcting their deficiencies.*

Feeling inspired, I decided to peek at my natural strengths and talents. I learned that I fall under at least three of the 34 categories: BELIEF, COMMUN-ICATION, EMPATHY. The book provides bullet point definitions and tips on how to maximize and harness your natural talents and strengths. So, for example, being a Communicator, I learned the following: *You like to explain, to describe, to host, to speak in public. You will always do well in jobs that require you to capture people's attention. Keep getting smarter about the words you use. They are a critical currency. And because you're so great, others like inviting you to social gatherings, dinners or events.*

The above is just one of the categories I fall under. Learning this got me really excited about being ME! So why not turn up the volume on the best of me and mute any self-doubt or speech that deflates my spirit?

I suggest that you, the reader, take a deeper look inside your water well. You might find a pail full of natural gifts and talents. I encourage you to tap this water source. You're sure to find not just one, but several areas of strength.

The aforementioned guide is actually a sub-clip of a management book titled, *Now, Discover your Strengths*. So, if manager-types have access to this information, why can't non-management persons also benefit from the philosophy and strategies of strengthening ourselves?

Look inside your well and fill your bucket with the best of you. And splash it onto life, over and over again. Do this with conviction. Forget about the self-doubt that's been gurgling in your mind. Own and celebrate YOU!

FINDING OUR FEATHERS

≈

One day, while walking in The Arts District of L.A., I nearly stepped on a white feather. Undaunted by street traffic on Santa Fe Avenue, I studied my find. Staring at the clouds, I gave into my pondering. *Hmm, a feather. I wonder if it's a feather I lost along the way. Or did it come from a fellow human, who's lost their passion to fly, whose wings have been clipped?*

I wondered if the feather came from a bird or a human. After all, we humans have inner wings. Like fowls, we too can (symbolically) lose feathers. Oftentimes, the only witness to this sorrowful occasion is our dreary heart.

Does it hurt when birds lose feathers? I know that when humans lose feathers, like losing a dream, it hurts. The whole image of a feather being so far apart from its home left me feeling melancholy. It reminded me of when things break such as: friendships, marriages…or the self.

Yes, our dreams have feathers too. Sometimes, people and circumstances clip our feathers. Ouch! Sometimes, our spirits start losing their elasticity and the feathers become dry, like brittle branches that break easily in the wind of a new season.

If you pull off a bird's feather, *yes*, it hurts them. But sometimes, as a way of life, feathers fall. I have read that just as we have bad hair days, birds also have bad feather days. Nature.org tells us that feathers are a bird's defining feature. But feathers wear out quickly and, in order to maintain peak performance, birds molt. They replace old feathers with new feathers at least once a year.

Back to the feather on Santa Fe Avenue. I wondered why it was there, all by itself, on this uneventful stretch of road. It was within a quarter mile of so much: downtown L.A. high rises, City Hall, skid row, Disney Hall, the Fashion District, Union Station. Yet, no one was around to catch it or notice it fall. There was absolutely no way this feather would ever make its way home. Sometimes our feathers never make their way home. Sometimes, in life's molting process, we form new feathers: new dreams, new friendships, new paths.

I have heard of people collecting feathers as a hobby. I imagine that said collectors feel incredibly jubilant when they happen upon a new feather. They might even add color to the feather, to jazz it up in peacock fashion.

Curiously, I looked up the meaning of white feathers. I learned from www.finefeatherheads.com that white feathers are a sign of angelic presence and divine guidance. They symbolize peace, love, protection, and light. "Finding a white feather is a powerful message and blessing from the Divine and is a sign that all will be right for you soon."

I have also read that feathers represent strength and growth. We might not be able to re-attach lost feathers, but we can open our plumage to newly discovered feathers. They may carry messages of new hopes and dreams. Perhaps they could teach us a new way of flying.

WORDS AND WARM SOCKS

≈

Don't ever diminish the power of words.
Words move hearts and hearts move limbs.

-Hamza Yusuf

When my oldest daughter, Gabby, was in kindergarten, she had a very caring and empathetic babysitter. And on cold mornings, before school, Tia Teresa would go out of her way to keep Gabby's feet warm. She would blow warm air into Gabby's socks, before slipping on her shoes. It was Tia's way of ensuring Gabby was off to a warm start.

When a teenager, my son Adam really enjoyed eating hot chicken soup. I would remind him to blow cool air onto his spoon. Mouth burns are no fun.

It is interesting how we can use our mouths to blow both hot and cool air. We seem to instinctively know how to compress the air, transforming warm breath into cool.

One Saturday afternoon, I shared this observation with my niece's daughter, Gigi. I stretched our conversation by asking the six-year-old if she could think of other ways that we can harness the breeze from our mouths. Without much hesitation, Gigi offered,

"Whistle! We can whistle." Raising her hand excitedly, Gigi went on, "Bubbles! We can also blow bubbles!"

I began contemplating other examples of dichotomy from the same source. I homed in on my favorite: **words**.

When we string words into sentences, energized words can have the power to lift, inspire, comfort, encourage, motivate or heal. But words can also form daggers. Words can equally hurt, humiliate, incite, trigger, break, anger, or crush a person.

Words are like eggs dropped from great heights;
you can no more call them back
than ignore the mess they leave when they fall.
-Jodi Picoult

How we string words is a decision made by our brains. Our brains are the vortex of our thoughts. And our words are the flute of our thoughts. In some cases, that flute can be more like a megaphone. Yikes! The poet Rumi reminds us that even softly spoken words can electrify.

Raise your words, not your voice.
It is rain that grows flowers, not thunder.
-Rumi

Yes, it is important to think before we speak and best to mind our words when angry with neighbor, relative or co-worker. Let us glance back at the vortex of words: the thoughts in our brain. The thoughts and words we choose about ourselves can be just as important as the words we use with others.

If we use better words when we speak to ourselves or about ourselves, we will lather our minds with positivity. Self-speak can reshape how we see ourselves in this world. If we paint ourselves with sunnier colors and adjectives, we might remold our outlook on life. Positivity can be contagious. Why not be a "superspreader" of positive words?

When canoeing in self-doubt or low self-esteem, we can start to sink. Why not be preventive with the words and thoughts we utter to ourselves? We can choose words that oil our minds. We have the power to refurnish your headspace.

There is a line in a Jack Johnson song, **Radiate**, which makes simple sense. It reminds us that we walk into the world we make. So, why not create a world in which you love all the furniture pieces?

PET ROCKS

≈

I met a smart, but odd girl at a Comfort Inn hotel many years ago. I was in the pool area with my two daughters when this girl sparked a conversation – very talkative, by the way. Her name is Paisley. Paisley's little sister's name is Peanut, *but dad likes to call her Christine*. She says she probably has an older sister that she hasn't met yet. Then, she told us about her pet rocks. Here's how the conversation went:

Paisley: I have three pet rocks. Do you want one?

Me: Well, aren't they special to you? Don't you want to keep them?

Paisley: One is named Hopper, the other one is named Jumper, and the other one I call Ready-ing.

Me: Red ears???

Paisley: No, Ready-ing...you know like ready, set, go. Ready! Ready-ing.

Me: Why did you name it that?

Paisley: Because it's readying for something... something really big and important. Just like me. I'm going to be involved in something really important someday, and I'm getting ready for it.

Me: How about the other rocks?

Paisley: They're just happy with where they are, but sometimes when nobody's looking, one jumps and the other hops. They're good friends.

Me: But you have a little sister. Isn't she your friend?

Paisley: Mom says she's my student. That's why I need to try not to…not to lie.

Me: Well, I certainly don't want to take your friends, the pet rocks, away from you. But thanks for offering.

Paisley: I was actually trying to sell you one.

That conversation with Paisley stands as one of my favorite conversations ever. Because from the start, I didn't know what she was going to say. She was like a good, simple and unpredictable movie that left you wondering.

Will young Paisley be involved in something big and important? Did she end up selling one or all of her pet rocks? Is Paisley a great teacher to her little sister, Christine, whom she calls Peanut?

Life can be like an unpredictable movie, filled with unique characters who add spark and funkiness. Our brains are all wired differently; they are coated with varying life experiences, speed bumps and adaptations. Regardless of our situation, we have an opportunity to dream big – all we have to do is be ready for it. Let's be like Paisley's third rock, always Ready-ing for something.

WHEN LIFE LACKS LUSTER

≈

One summer day, I opened my laptop to write a piece on how, at times, it's okay to find oneself in a state of idleness. It is okay, I would write, to accept that there are times when life seems uneventful, dull, or even perhaps lacking a boost of forward-arching dreams and objectives. WAIT A MINUTE! There is nothing about life that is dull, not even in the quiet in-betweens. Yes, there are times when the day is more sedate than others, but this does not mean that the stars inside of us, and outside of us, have stopped twinkling.

Some of us tend to experience anxiety when our spirits appear to be in an idle state.

My son, Adam, was on school break that same summer. He spent a couple of weeks lacking routine. I mentioned that he seemed depressed. Adam said there was nothing exciting in his life. He felt unaccomplished, unmotivated and dull. I explained that he was just experiencing summertime blues and reminded him that if he paid attention to everything around him – as well as inside him – he would have little reason to feel dull. Miracles are uprising all around us.

Some of us don't know how to handle the quiet times, so we sort of start to hyperventilate. Gasping for air, reaching for any distraction that will quell the stillness. Could it be because in stillness, our thoughts are much louder? Perhaps some thoughts are distressing, carrying memories that ache or diminish us. So then, we start reaching for branches that might keep us from drowning in unknown waters. Perhaps we panic, wanting to remain relevant and purposeful.

Instead, try asking yourself, *when is life lackluster, dull or slow?* Even when it appears life has no momentum, the engines are revving full throttle inside of us.

How can our lives ever be idle, when we have millions of cells, countless transmitters, heavy-duty organs, feet, hands, brains working in unison? These are all exciting miracles contained in our powerful locomotive vessel, our bodies, our minds, our intellect, our caring hearts. We are more powerful than intermittent thoughts or concerns about stagnancy.

If that's not enough, if we look outside our immediate shell, there is so much going on that keeps us alive. We have the power of the sun, moon and gravity, all pulling for us. As explained in nasa.gov, gravity is what holds the planets in orbit around the sun, and gravity keeps the moon in orbit around Earth. The gravitational pull of the moon pulls the seas towards it, causing the ocean tides. Gravity creates stars and planets by pulling together the material from which they are made. These are just a few things keeping life in balance. It all appears seamless, so much so that we may take these things for granted.

Understanding the enormity of our universe, and our role in it, is exciting stuff. This opens a window and an invitation to fly higher. Once we truly grasp the reality of our greatness, our eyes can widen, and our wings expand ascending from dull to extraordinary skies.

I think of a young man with a roaring voice. On occasion, this young man would visit our church, take the mic and sing. His voice is deep, powerful, soulful, a true gift. Sitting in the audience and listening to him sing, it was impossible to ignore the magic that sprung from his well.

At a church celebration one night, the mic was passed around and congregants shared a little bit of testimony. When the mic came to this singer, he said he does not believe in being ordinary. He pointed to his mother sitting next to him, "You listen to her, and you see her, she's blind. So, it is impossible for me to be ordinary if this woman is my mother. I aim to be extraordinary. That is what God created in me. So, if he created me, I honor him by being the best of what he created in me."

This young man's words stuck, reminding me to be grand in everything. Why not be bold in everything we do? In doing so, we can reflect the ocean that swirls inside us. Why opt to be dull, deflated and ordinary, when we can aim to be extraordinary?

FLAP YOUR WINGS
AND TAKE A POWER NAP

≈

I re-read a slice of writing from 10 years ago. Within that five-lined poem, I bemoaned being *tired of crying about being tired*. I was divorced and mom to three grown children at the time. My poem zigzagged from complaining about being physically exhausted to feeling empowered by my independent wings. While my writing entry reminded me of how I had thoroughly embraced being single, the last line on my slim note perplexed me, "Even wings get tired."

That got me wondering about our winged friends, birds; do these tiny pilots get tired when flying? I found out that birds actually rarely get tired. Their bodies are structured in a way, that they can actually nap while flying. Some call it "power napping".

Birds are astounding. We can certainly pluck lessons from the way they navigate life. An article on chipperbirds.com explains a bird's flying endurance. Birds have a unique ability to control the speed and frequency of their wingbeats. This allows them to conserve energy over long distances. Hollow bones help reduce energy needed for flying – air resistance is also critical. Birds' streamlined body shape allows them to cut through the air with minimal resistance. They can also change the shape of their wings to alter their flight path and reduce drag.

I centered on the term "wingbeats." Apparently, the fewer wingbeats needed, the better. Birds use a combination of gliding and flapping flight, switching between the two to maintain altitude and speed.

When I hear the word "wingbeats," I cannot help but think of "heartbeats," which brings me to our most tender spot: our hearts.

When we are physically or mentally tired, I imagine that the rhythm of our hearts alters. Exhaustion can make our hearts beat faster, or slower. Perhaps this is a time to step in and assist the gliding process.

I assume that most of us, on occasion, have seen multiple heavy packages drop onto our doorstep. Managing multiple problems or concerns can appear impossible. Best to tackle them one step at a time. Sometimes, it helps to step back, take a deep breath…and a nap. I have found that a power nap can help reshape our wings and reduce the emotional drag.

The idea of "power naps" was coined by Professor James Maas, while at Cornell University. Maas is the CEO of Sleep for Success; he has also written several books, including, "Sleep Power." Maas says that the benefits of power naps include the restoring of alertness, performance, and learning ability. Naps are also good for the heart.

The term "power naps" rings similar to the word "siesta." The site slumberwise.com explains that siestas originated in Spain. The name siesta is derived from the Latin: hora sexta, meaning the sixth hour.

Traditionally, the day's hours began at dawn, so the sixth hour would be noon – a great time for a nap.

Power naps and siestas are intended to recharge us, to reset our brains. Power naps are also good for our heartbeats (wingbeats). When you find yourself exhausted physically, mentally or emotionally, why not pause and recharge? Which is exactly what I did while finishing up this writing piece.

It was around noon. I was at a coffee shop, when suddenly I felt an urge to rest. My creative juices ran low. I could not think of a clever way to end this chapter on power naps. So, I drove home, listened to sounds of water trickling down a river on my phone, and napped for a few minutes.

After my nap, I decided to end this story by laying down the truth: naps help.

Painting Over Walls and Your Ex's Tattoo

≈

Dutch visual artist, Lilly Van Der Stokker, prefers walls over canvas. Working from home, she likes to paint on her walls. Van Der Stokker told Talk Art – a podcast revolving around the world of art – that when she completes a painting, she simply photographs it. The photographs transform into prints. When Van Der Stokker is inspired or ready to begin a new project, she paints over the same wall. So, the original paintings start getting tucked away in the past.

Listening to Van Der Stokker talk so nonchalantly about painting over an existing art piece was difficult to conjure. If I had the ability to paint an extraordinary piece, I would certainly want to preserve it for as long as possible.

After reflecting on Van Der Stokker's unique approach, I wondered *what is the longest existing artwork?* While there has been much debate about the oldest artwork, artnet.com tells us that some archaeologists believe the world's oldest-known representational artwork is that of three wild pigs painted deep in a limestone cave on the Indonesian island of Sulawesi at least 45,500 years ago. The ancient images, first reported in the journal Science Advances, were found in Leang Tedongnge cave. The artwork was made with red ochre pigment. The painting appears to depict a group of Sulawesi warty pigs, two of which appear to be fighting. Researchers were apparently blown away by the finding – one described the image as the most spectacular and well-preserved figurative animal paintings known from the whole region.

If I could paint over anything, I would splash a giant paint brush over bad memories. Yes, I can think of a few relics I would drop into the abyss. Would it not be interesting if we could easily paint over things that have caused us pain or distress? Say for example, a traumatic event or a failed relationship that overwhelms our spirit?

History is important. There have been atrocities committed against races and religions. Those types of deep wounds cannot be painted over. There also exist experiences filed in our personal cabinets that help us make better decisions moving forward. So, it can be important to access those lessons.

However, there are some experiences that might benefit from some cloaking over with a new quart of paint. I surmise that, at one point or another, we have all been wronged. While some of us are able to put those wrongs behind us and move forward, others cannot. I know a young man who routinely brings up the past. Like a crutch, he leans on his past; he often brings up situations in which a certain person has injured or betrayed him. His past trails behind him, as if it were part of his identity. He carries a U-Haul of wrongs.

I suggest that, on occasion, we take ourselves to the "emotional" home improvement store. Why not pick up a new can of paint and start fresh? Take snapshots of the good memories and hold on to those – then stroke a new day with a healthy brush.

I suspect that some failed relationships are difficult to paint over; it can be impossible to pretend they didn't exist or matter much. Consequently, what if there are physical reminders that trigger us, like a tattoo bearing the name or initials of an ex-partner? Well, we certainly cannot take a paint brush to our skin. But there is a work-around.

Tattoo artists can work magic with an unwanted tattoo bearing an ex's name. Removery.com tells us that a tattoo artist can often use the existing linework within a new design. Fading an ex's tattoo name is the first step. Once the linework has been lightened, it can be repurposed. Namery.com suggests that if the ex's tattoo name is very small, it can be easily worked into a small part of a new design, like the leaf of a flower. Other cover-up designs include a frog, spider and an owl. I particularly like one coverup design. Removery.com shows a bee covering up an ex-boyfriend's name. Reminding the person that "You'll BEE alright."

RUNNING THROUGH SPRINKLERS

CONNECTING WITH OTHERS

PART 3

Running Through Sprinklers

≈

When my daughter Gabby was six years old, we drove out to a park in a neighboring town. I had driven past this park on occasion and noticed kids happily running through the sprinklers and simply enjoying outdoor play. The park would be a welcome relief for an exceptionally hot summer day. It offered plenty of shade and boasted an above-the-head sprinkler system. As we settled in at the park that day, I searched for a shady place under which to sit. I encouraged Gabby to join in on the water fun. Within a minute of finding the perfect bench, I turned my attention back to the play area. I saw an image that would plant itself in my "happiest memories" vault.

What I saw that afternoon had me break into pregnant laughter. To my surprise, my friendly little Gabby was already joyfully running through the curtains of water. The most surprising part of this sight was that Gabby was running through while holding hands with another little girl, a complete stranger. There she was, my bubbly Gabby, in all her splendor beaming a huge smile and gurgling happy giggles as she ran through the sprinklers. I had been well aware of

Gabby's friendly and outgoing demeanor; she was quick at making friends. Seeing her, within such a short time, holding hands with a complete stranger, and loving it…well, this made me fall in love with her even more. That memory stands as one of my all-time favorite moments. A spontaneous, uninhibited connection. Two happy souls enjoying life's happy gifts.

The term "stranger danger" was particularly en vogue during Gabby's grammar school years. But on that particular summer day, all concerns went out the window. I absolutely loved experiencing it. Would our world not be better if we, like park playgrounds, had no walls – if we could easily reach out and hold a friendly hand? Similarly, can you imagine starting a new job, and having a co-worker offer to hold your hand and tour you around?

My late friend, Scott Spiro, was a gentle soul who went out of his way to fold in others. At his funeral, at least two co-workers talked about how, on their first day on the job, it was Scott who extended a hand and offered to help in any way. He was friendly and reassuring. Both speakers would never forget that experience, especially so because they were a little intimidated and hesitant on their first day. Reaching out to a new classmate, new neighbor or co-worker can make a difference that could last a lifetime.

As an adult, Gabby works in a field where she recruits and includes others. A perfect match for a girl who doesn't hesitate to lend a welcoming hand, while beaming a reassuring smile. Just like those water sprinklers, she routinely splashes uninhibited jolliness.

Popping Out of Life's Car

≈

Standing in line for my latte, I eavesdropped on a conversation between a woman, her young son and daughter, and another customer. They were talking about the recent loss of a pet. Then out of nowhere, the boy offered up, "I was five days early. I came out of my dad's car!"

Everyone chuckled. Mom, containing her laughter, watery-eyed, blushed, "Well, that's a whole 'nother story."

Most of us are familiar with the abbreviated version of the birds and the bees, "You came out of your mom's tummy." But the boy's version sounded a little different.

I couldn't help but ask. Did I hear correctly, your son came out of his dad's car?

The family felt bouncy enough to share more details. The family lived ten blocks from the hospital. Since mom's first child labor lasted almost two days, the family figured they had plenty of time, as the contractions progressed. They only made it to the hospital parking lot. The baby boy literally popped out of his dad's car.

We all laughed for a while. I suggested to the boy, well maybe this will transcend to your professional life, you can show up to work early every day. Mom affirmed, "Oh yes, they are both true to core. She's steady and patient. He's very enthusiastic and always ready."

My middle daughter, Amanda, was hesitant at birth. Even with induced labor, she held out as long as she could. She waited 28 hours before peering out into the world. Her birth also reflects her tentative personality. I call her my worry bird. In fact, I often asked her to hand me her worries so that I could place them in my pocket.

I am not an expert in the formation of personalities. But as a mother of three and an adamant observer of people, I do have some thoughts on the matter.

I have always gotten a kick from watching children maneuver life. You see all kinds of personalities on the playground: the kid who does not like sharing; the kid who wants everyone to get along; the kid who steps in and sets up park rules. There are kids who climb up the slide instead of coming down on it. I love the kids who go fast on the swing and then jump off. Then there is the kid who is okay being alone, enjoying the subtle motion of a bouncy horse.

From life observations, I discern that we stay pretty close to the skin we had on, when we break out from our cocoon. We enter this world with our embedded DNA, our personalities, and physiology. Then we take our rhythm into a large, scary, beautiful, complex world. This world, our environment, and our tribe help shape, prune, and sometimes dent us. We are a mix and match of personalities, gifts, talents, and some hardships.

For a college summer research class, my son Adam and his lab colleagues each worked on creating a unique molecule. I could never do that. As I drive past large construction sites, I watch workers in orange vests create colossal structures; I can't do that. I wish I could create an app, but I can't do that. I also know that I have skills and talents that mix well with the cocktail of life.

I was born in a house, on a small ranch. A midwife helped deliver me. I can tell you one thing, I entered this world with humility, and I hope to leave this world with that same humility. Whether you popped up out of a car in a parking lot, landed in a comfortable hospital setting, or were born in a house or hut, be you. We have no control of how we enter this world. However, we can always spruce up our pre-programmed personalities and gifts to help enrich the way we engage with others. We all play a role in steadying life's teeter totter. As for the selfish kid on the playground, well, I have met lots of YOUs, and I still love you.

Keep Your Pants to Yourself

Tips on doing laundry…

≈

Three hours into my work shift, I left my desk for a cup of tea. As I walked the hallway toward the office kitchen, I casually stuck a hand inside my pants right pocket. I was surprised to feel how deep, into the pocket, my arm dropped. Literally, my pants pocket swallowed a significant portion of my arm, just below my elbow. I laughed at the situation. *I never knew these pockets could be so deep!* By the time I made it back to my desk, giggling, I realized that I was actually wearing my son's pants.

Laughing wholeheartedly, I shared the revelation with my co-workers. *How could this even happen!* I surmised that when doing laundry a few days prior, I had mixed up Adam's navy blue pants with my own dark blue pants. Today, in my usual morning haste, I neglected to check myself in the mirror.

Sometimes, when we mix laundry, things can get a little messy. Neutrals can take on different hues, garments can end up in someone else's closet or drawers. We can even end up in someone else's pants.

This got me thinking about other potential mix-ups. For example, when connecting with one another and lending an ear to another's problems, we might also end up mixing their laundry (problems) with our own. We could end up carting somebody's heavy load.

I spend a lot of time listening to friends and family, as they sift through problems or dilemmas. I typically don't mind lending support or giving advice. But I deliberately arm myself with boundaries and make a cognizant effort not to take on the other person's problems. I try to keep my laundry separate.

There are ways to listen, empathize, discern, comfort and give advice to friends – without taking on their loads. Unfortunately, not everyone observes laundry room etiquette. You may have experienced this yourself. There are some who overlook boundaries and blur the wash, while others might not hesitate mixing their blues with yours.

A friend recently shared a quote from writer Octavia Raheem:

Folks who don't have honor or maintain their own boundaries have no capacity to respect yours. They haven't built that inner muscle. If we are not mindful, the lack of boundaries spills into interactions – tries to become a force, banging up against your sanity integrity, relationship…all the things.

Raheem explains that when she observes someone leaking out their emotions – unconsciously or consciously, offering their mess – she bears witness, acknowledges what's going on and doesn't make anyone good, bad, worse or better. She inhales, exhales and quietly says to herself, *"None of that leakage is mine nor will become mine."*

In other words, don't take ownership of another person's problems. Protect your peace. Having said that, there may be times when you're stirred to do a little more to lighten someone's load; it's all about balance.

For her second birthday, my daughter Gabby was quick to pick out one of her favorite party gifts. Her aunt Blanca gave Gabby a shopping cart with make-believe groceries. During the party, Gabby joyfully pushed the tiny shopping cart around the yard. At one point, Gabby hit a crack in the driveway. Her shopping cart got stuck and wouldn't make it over the hump. I watched, curious to see how long it would take Gabby to back up the cart and go around the buckled cement. Uncle Peter happened to be walking by and quickly lifted the shopping cart and placed it away from the cracked cement. Gabby went on her merry way. Peter looked at me with a questioning gesture. Peter intervened, and I chose to be an observant cheerleader.

Whose approach was the correct one in this situation, mine or Peter's? Maybe the right answer is somewhere in between. In being there for others, maybe we can provide advice in the form of a question, "I wonder what would happen if you pulled the cart back a little?" Or perhaps we can provide information that can empower the person and motivate them to find his or her own way through the haze.

We can be there for others, support, give counsel, without taking on their load. Remember, it's important to keep enough fuel in your own tank. Boundaries can help keep our own laundry a bit more tidy.

RUNNING THE MILE-Y CYRUS

≈

When I was in middle school, I was voted "Craziest" for our yearbook's 'Hall of Fame.' My best friend, Teresa, was voted "Best Hair Style." We laughed at ourselves for the funky labels we had earned. Come picture day for the Hall-of-Famers, we were more than ready to wink for the camera. Regrettably, our block of time for picture day would follow our PE class. That presented a problem.

As we styled our hair and adjusted light make up that morning, neither Teresa nor I knew that we would be asked to run the mile during PE that afternoon. Our PE class would precede our photo session. Yikes!

So, we tried to work around this.

Our PE teacher, Mr. Gropack, was firm on what he expected from students. That afternoon, Mr. Gropack divided the class. One group of students would run the mile, while the others would make their way to the gym for weight training. The groups would then alternate halfway through the period. Secretly, Teresa and I mischievously plotted. We would "walk" the mile, as to not disturb our hairstyle and makeup. *Mr. Gropack would never know*. Little did we know that Mr. Gropack had a direct view of the track from an upstairs weight room window. Uh oh.

He made us run the mile twice.

I was immature and could only think of one emotion aimed at Mr. Gropack: hatred. That day, I resisted running the mile. For most of my remaining semester, I resisted respecting or appreciating Mr. Gropack. (although eventually Mr. Gropack came to respect me despite a twisted avenging prank I pulled on him, but that's for another book).

Nowadays, when I spot a running track, I'm often reminded of those silly middle school days when my resistance to the mile often emerged. With the exception of avid runners, I am certain that many peers also begrudged running the mile.

I got to thinking about other things that we resist. For example, getting older.

The singer, Miley Cyrus, has been known for resisting and rebelling against labels. She fought hard against being kept in specific music genres. She wanted to sing to the sound of her own drum…or guitar.

I enjoy some of her songs, like "Flowers." I also like her summer 2023 single, "Used to be Young." The once rebellious songstress is not resisting getting older; she's graciously appreciating what shaped her into who she is now, and she seems fine with it.

Running the mile in PE and growing older have one thing in common: they are assigned prerequisites – you can't avoid them. In her single, Cyrus sings that she's had a good run. In accepting the course of life, the artist has learned to run with the flow. So, why not you? I am not advising against fighting the important fights, resisting unfairness and mistreatment, but perhaps you can choose your battles. There are some things we can't avoid. So why not lean into this acceptance and do like Miley, run the mile-y Cyrus?

EMOTIONAL HITCHHIKERS

≈

Have you ever picked up a hitchhiker? Perhaps. I am not referring to your average hitchhiker here. I am talking about emotional hitchhikers – unwelcome guests who latch on and disrupt the balance of one's personal load.

When I was a child, I lived on a small farm in Mexico. Back then, owning a car was a luxury – I was fortunate to have relatives who owned vehicles. I recall being a frequent passenger in the back of my uncle's truck. One time, as my uncle's truck came to a rolling stop on a dirt road, three men unexpectedly hopped onto the cab. They were unsought hitchhikers, but not necessarily brutes. These were average townspeople who stood under the shade of a tree, waiting for the infrequent bus. There was only one bus to serve our small town.

Because the bumpy dirt roads forced cars to slow, these uninvited hitchhikers took advantage of the break and hopped on. My uncle shrugged off the inconvenience, tilted his sombrero and kept driving. When our truck neared the group's destination, with a slight pound to the side of the truck, the men jumped off. They simply hollered a pleasantry, "Gracias. A la otra!" *Thank you, see you next time.*

Do you know that just as these men used folksiness to strong-arm a ride, there are individuals who are more than ready to drop their emotional load onto our cab? I call them emotional hitchhikers. They are not necessarily bad people; they are simply looking for reprieve. Sometimes their approach is veiled. Other times, one can clearly see what's lurking. Thumbs out. Their hitchhiking can come in the form of a phone call, text message or other. They want to vent; they need advice; they want to "unload".

Yes, it's nice to help a friend, relative or neighbor when possible. However, it is important to recognize when your load is already too heavy. Why not give yourself permission to decline some calls or not respond to a disquieting message?

Expanding on this notion a little, let us consider social media. Random or deliberate posts can also bear resemblance to emotional hitchhikers. Sometimes, clicking on a negative, angry, or derogatory post can entangle us emotionally. Unintentionally, we choose to open the door and take on somebody else's emotional debris. There are individuals who are unable to discern emotion or space, so they recruit the attention of others on social media. Do not take that ride.

I am an advocate of being there for others. However, I routinely work at protecting my peace and balance. I have eaten at restaurants where an overextended employee, attempting to balance a platter, has dropped and broken a plate or two. They likely picked up more than their platter could hold. Let us be mindful to not carry more than we can handle.

Sometimes it is okay to bypass an emotional hitchhiker. Align your wheels and stay on course. Be a friend, lend a caring hand, or even an ear. But do so on your terms and when your own road is not too bumpy.

IF YOU LOST FAITH, CALL 1 (888)…

≈

Goodbyes are only for those who love with their eyes. Because for those who love with heart and soul there is no such thing as separation.

- Rumi

So, you woke up to see another day. What will you do with it?

In early 2021, I was driving on Santa Fe Avenue in Downtown Los Angeles and happened to glance up at a billboard. "If you have lost faith in God, call (888)…." I contemplated, knowing that the message resonated. Yes, I had lost faith.

Our season of loss had leaked into another year. The pandemic continued its indiscriminate gnawing at life. In the midst of sorrow, I watched friends drift away from their faith – I also witnessed some of the holy become holier. Then there were the in-betweeners, like me. It is a horrible thing to feel and worse yet to write what I was feeling back then. I was holding a grudge against God.

I had not attended church service since the start of the pandemic. At first, the excuses were social distancing, slow the spread efforts, etcetera. But the real reason for skipping Sunday service was resentment. As death had taken a giant rake to the living, many of us were asking, *God, how can you let this happen?* Although this question burned inside me regularly, I continued to pray, and prayed really hard for loved ones struggling to stay alive.

Pivoting, I'm going to leave God out of this for a minute.

I have often said that the best way to live is to remember that we're going to die. I was reminded of this a few days after reading the billboard. Sadly, I attended my high school boyfriend's funeral. Seeing his larger-than-life smile on a photo poster, hearing the bagpipes play and watching the doves fly, the truth took to the megaphone: We are mortal. Life is temporary.

Death is not the greatest loss in life.
The greatest loss is what dies inside us while we live.

-Norman Cousins

The preacher asked funeral attendees, "What message would our friend have for us, now that he has seen a truth to which we are not yet privy?" The preacher answered his own question with three points: Life is short, forgive others, and live a life of service.

Regardless of the spiritual island you inhabit, today, I share a reminder: Our physical existence on this earth is temporary. We are all in the same boat. Some have lived kinder lives than others. Some have endured harsher lessons than others. Regardless of your circumstance, what will you do today that will make the most of your flame?

You CAN be Kind

≈

One summer, running errands took me to L.A.'s Skid Row. That day, a young man crossing the street ahead of me taught me a tender lesson in kindness.

With a limp in his walk, the young man used his left hand to hold up his over-sized, frayed pants. In his right hand, he held two smashed soda cans. Ahead of us, and coming in our direction, an elderly man carried a large bag of recyclables. I was taken aback when the younger man politely offered his two cans to the older gentleman, whose bag was already plenty full. The young man, bowing, humbly offered, "Here you go…for you."

I witnessed this person selflessly give all he had to another, who obviously had more. The older man appeared surprised, but smiled warmly, *for me?* This young man's actions embodied a mixture of kindness, respect and politeness.

The word polite comes from the Latin word politus, which means polished: made smooth, refined, elegant. That summer day, I had not suspected I would find such elegance on Skid Row.

When I reflect on the word **polite**, I think about kindness, respect, compassion, humility. Acts that honor the spirit of politeness can provide a ray of hope. If more of us do our part to create these rays, then perhaps our communal light can guide us to one another.

I lean on the words of French moralist and essayist Joseph Joubert:

Politeness is the flower of humanity.

Perhaps today is a good day to kindly share a flower with a neighbor.

BE STILL OUR TONGUES

≈

It was Sunday, in the middle of June, our church prayer sheets came around. Someone, pointing toward a blind woman sitting next to me, handed me a clipboard and said, "Can you write down her prayer request? She'll tell it to you."

I turned to the blind woman and offered to write her prayer. She said, "Ask the church to pray for me, for my two daughters, and for my granddaughter." I thought she was finished, but she added, "And pray that...be still my tongue".

Brother Tom, who reads all the prayer requests, nodded as he proceeded, "Sister Mary, I know what you're talking about. Sweet and sour water does not come from the same river."

Although in practical terms, Brother Tom is right, I disagree somewhat. By guilty admission, I have indeed allowed both sweet and sour to flow out of my river. Sister Mary inspired me to police my own tongue.

On another church occasion, a friend, Mr. Harris, handed me a couple of pamphlets and a picture button. The button read, "Peace starts with me." I quickly pinned it to my purse. What a wonderful reminder to be a source of peace, instead of firing bullets or setting off rockets. Amen!

Interesting to me how three senses came into play here. Sister Mary can't see (sense of sight), yet she's mindful of the words that others hear (sense of hearing). Nonetheless, her heart (which I call her sense of emotion) is able to contour both senses. Perhaps our hearts can serve as the best sensors; tenderly equipped to intercept stinging words.

HOLY GUACAMOLE

≈

I was known as the Donut Lady at a former workplace. Each Friday, I would bring in three boxes of donuts. I would also go the extra mile for some healthier co-workers by bringing bananas, apples, and a handful of avocados – I had actually formed a small avocado club at the office. One of the avocado recipients was not always in a friendly disposition. Regardless, my intention was to hoist my colleagues from the weight of their heavy workload. I did not discriminate.

One particular Friday, however, I was not inspired to give an avocado to this difficult recipient. They were being difficult. I was tempted to give them the smallest, and least ripe of the bunch. Instead, I gave them my best avocado.

I had read that the people whom we like the least, or whose personalities challenge us the most, are the ones whose stories we do not know. I remind myself of this often, especially at work. At one point, I actually armed myself with the book: "How to Hug a Porcupine." In fact, I kept it in my office drawer.

There are plenty of porcupines that hover in our world. Realistically, we cannot always facilitate a sit-down with every single one of them in order to "understand them better." However, we can remind ourselves that we are all part of the human fabric. We are all fragmented patches on the quilt of life. Although these porcupines might prod along on a patch way on the other side of our quilt, life's needle is always working to stitch us together.

So instead of reacting to the porcupines' negative energy or allowing them to vacuum us into their sunken dark caves, perhaps we can approach our foe with our best avocado. Imagine this: putting an avocado in between you and the porcupine in your life. Then… SQUEEZE! Holy Guacamole!

A note to consider from untamedanimals.com, which points out that baby porcupines (Porcupettes) are soft and made of hardened hair so that their mother doesn't get hurt during birth. The quills will harden within hours of birth. Maybe we are all born soft…and life circumstances harden our quills.

NAME YOUR PILLAR

≈

Who's your pillar?

My daughter, Amanda, works with troubled teens. Her empathetic nature and wisdom make her a natural counselor. When Amanda started a post-graduate job, she began calling me more often. I never mind hearing from her. When she's had a rough day, she reaches out to me. I am always prepared to listen and share advice, ready to be her pillar. Consequently, Amanda spends each of her workdays being a pillar for others.

I observe that in this climb we call life, we take turns holding each other up. We take turns being a pillar to those who need uplifting.

A pillar is defined as a person or thing regarded as reliably providing essential support for something. A pillar can be called Amanda, Suzie, or Joe. Pillars can have names, literally.

In the Bible, 1 Chronicles tells us about the building of God's Temple by Solomon. The Temple was built by thousands of men and was covered in gold. One of the most impressive features of the Temple were two pillars that stood at the porch of the Temple. I found it interesting that each pillar was given a name. The one to the right was named Jachin, and the one on the left was named Boaz. It is said that the pillars were named after King David and his son Solomon.

Who or what has been your pillar lately? If you find yourself feeling pillar-less, perhaps you can be a pillar to someone else.

FOIL PAPER IN MICROWAVE

≈

My mom was 88 when she visited me during the summer of 2023. She watched me from my living room as I pulled leftovers from my fridge to reheat in the microwave. Through my peripheral vision, I could see her shoulders lift a little as she spoke, "You know, if you put foil paper in the microwave, it can explode or cause a fire."

With squinting eyes and pursed lips, I responded to her good intentions, "Mom, I'm a 58-year-old woman, do you think that I don't already know this? I have warmed up lots of meals in the microwave. I learned about the foil paper thing many, many years ago." Slightly dismissive she added, "I was just making sure."

I think it was within hours of the microwave pep talk that mom shared another piece of advice, "You know, eating fruits and vegetables are good for your health." God, love her. I love her.

My college-aged son, Adam, was also visiting me that summer. I was astonished when I heard myself talking to Adam the same way my mom had been talking to me, sharing life advice with a kind of urgency.

My mother is elderly and fragile, struggling with mobility issues. Her health is certainly a concern. Perhaps we are both simply trying to prepare our children for life, knowing that we will not always be there to guide them. As Adam continues college and becomes more independent, spending the majority of his time away from home, perhaps I feel an urgency to say as much as I can before he fully dives into life's giant bowl. Similarly, perhaps my mother is sharing as much as she can, before her body and mind lose access to her children.

While I found myself trying not to be like my mother, to not smother my son with limitless advice, I also found myself empathizing and understanding my mother a little better.

Her advice continued in my backyard, "You know, you should cut the dry branches from your lime tree, so that it stays healthy and produces more fruit." Advice well taken.

A few days later, Adam was about to walk out our front door wearing a particularly wrinkled shirt. Like Adam, I am not a fan of the iron. So, I suggested, "You know, if you get a damp cloth or t-shirt and throw it in the dryer with the wrinkled shirt, it will soften the wrinkles."

I watched Adam leave the house wearing a completely different shirt. Hmm.

Some things stick, other things don't. My eggs sometimes stick to the pan – which reminds me of the most outlandish advice from my mom. I was getting ready to mix a few eggs in a bowl. "You need to crack the eggs first," she contributed.

The advice we mommas give may not always be eggcellent, but it does come from a nest of good intentions. I realize that we're simply trying to prune out the dry branches, so our children live bountiful and fruitful lives.

DETERMINED HAPPY MEAL

≈

What makes us unstoppable? Keeping our eyes on the prize can certainly fuel our determination. Just as a baseball player can jump extra feet to catch a deep outfield ball, our perseverance can overtake barriers.

When my son Adam was about 5-years old, we stopped for lunch at McDonalds. We ate our food in the indoor playground area – he loved going down the slide and tumbling in the soft padding and plastic balls.

That day, a woman and her three kids sat next to us. One boy was about Adam's age, another boy appeared to be about 13 years old, and lastly a toddler girl. These kids ate their happy meals and grabbed the toy trucks inside their happy bags. They placed the toy trucks at the top of a slide and watched the trucks roll down at a pretty fast pace. At one point, the older boy's truck flipped and went over and into a meshed bar. With lament, we all watched the truck drop into an unreachable area.

After some attempts at reaching the toy, the mom summoned an employee for assistance. The young worker looked at the group, then at the playground, focusing on the mesh between the toy and the people. "Sorry, we can't get to it."

The older boy was on the verge of tears. As I returned to my meal, I felt a breeze tickle my ears. Shockingly, the boy was running toward the contraption in tackle position and pushing his shoulder and right side of body into the mesh material. The material was firm and impenetrable. The boy's body bounced firmly back. The boy, undeterred, went back a few feet and again, tackled the apparatus. I worried that he might break a bone or injure his shoulder. I watched him do this four times. The mom made him stop. An employee came out with a key and opened the backside of the apparatus, reaching down for the toy truck and handing it to the mom in the group.

Many years later, I watched another determined young man. This time, I was hiking a challenging trail in Sierra Madre, California. As I made my way up, I noticed the young man, dressed in a black t-shirt and black shorts, pushing a bike uphill. There were many rocks along that portion of the trail. As I passed by him, I asked, "Are you going to ride that bike all the way downhill, with all the rocks?" He grinned, "I didn't realize it was going to be this challenging. It's my first time up here." I smiled. "Well, I've only seen one guy on a bike up here." Smirking, he said, "Well, now you've seen two."

I laughed and continued my hike but wondered, *he's already come up high enough, why doesn't he just turn around?*

I made it to a pretty high point, at which I typically stop and turn around. I could hear the biker huffing and puffing as he continued pushing his bike up. I admired his determination. "Wow, you're strong and determined."

The biker again said that he didn't realize how hard it was going to be. "But I have to keep going." The biker's focus was the spot on his cellphone: "You see, there's a spot up here. I came for the spot, to claim it. But it's pretty far up – I'm only about 300 meters away." The biker's focus was the spot on his cellphone. At the time, there was a popular *Pokemon Go* game that challenged players to physically make it to a designated spot on their phone to catch a Pokemon. That day's Pokemon was the biker's motivation. The steep, rocky climb did not deter him. The fact that he had to push his bike up also didn't stop him. He did not alter his plan. His unwavering eye was on the prize…on the Pokemon.

Life can detour our travels and block our destination or objective. But as it has been famously said, "Where there's a will, there's a way." Or perhaps, we can consider the words of motivational speaker Zig Zigler:

"When obstacles arise, you change your direction to reach your goal; you do not change your decision to get there."

LIFE IS GOOD

Tell it to the world!

≈

Waking up feeling motivated one St. Patrick's Day, I went for an early morning hike up Mt. Wilson trail in Sierra Madre, California. As I reached a midpoint, I turned a corner and came upon three men, two of them holding small dogs. The group smiled politely. The handsome one, in the middle, looked up from his dog and pleasantly nodded, "Life is good". I smiled back, "Yes, life is good." I wondered inwardly, *oouh, am I looking cute today*?

Before returning, I took it all in. The white, fluffy clouds had ushered clear blue skies, following overnight rain. The air was crisp and the whole mountain smelled fresh and clean.

As I headed down, I felt my smile widen effortlessly. I shared hearty pleasantries with fellow hikers. I maneuvered a few rocks, then turned my attention to a group of young men resting on a spot at the top of the "switchback" known as the *locks*. The men politely moved out of the way to let me through. I was taken aback when a young man, sitting on a large rock, also affirmed, "Life is good." I repeated back with a resolute, "Yes, life is good indeed."

I was thrilled by the positive energy emitting from the San Gabriel Mountains that day. These hikers were passing along the phrase "Life is Good." It was like a tag game of positivity. So, as I continued my descent, I decided that I would continue this tag game. Two women and several kids were hiking up. With an extra spring in my step and a confident smile, I repeated to them, "Life is good." The women side glanced each other, smiled apprehensively. One of them instructed the kids to stay away from the edge. *Hmm, maybe these ladies were not getting the whole positivity thing today.*

Regardless, as I drove home, I called one of my kids and started the conversation, "Life is good." My daughter, Gabby, responded, "What?" I suggested to Gabby that she repeat the phrase to a stranger. "Why not? It can't hurt to share positive words with complete strangers. Pass along positivity." I called my then boyfriend (now husband) and suggested the same thing. During the week, I also shared my "life is good" encounter with a friend and neighbor.

A couple of weeks later, I drove to my boyfriend's place. We were making our way out for a light hike, when my boyfriend looked up and smiled, affirming, "Life is Good." Perplexed, I tilted my head. David added clarity, "Your shirt. It says *life is good*."

Wouldn't you know it… I was wearing a green shirt with an imprint of the phrase, *Life is Good.* Yes, this was the same green shirt that I had worn on that St. Patrick's Day hike. Silly me, those hikers had simply been reading my shirt, "Life is good".

Well, what the heck. Why can't we start that positivity tagging game today, or any day? Repeat after me, "Life is good". Tell it to the world (friend, partner, co-worker, sibling), life is good!

ACKNOWLEDGEMENTS

This book would not have been possible without the inspiration and support of many wonderful people. I am deeply grateful to them all.

To my three amazing children, Gabby, Amanda, and Adam, who have filled my life with joy and wonder. You are the reason I write these stories. Your adventurous spirit and your courage to explore new horizons have motivated me to do the same. You are also kind, loving, resourceful, and hilarious. I love you more than words can say.

To the people who helped me polish and improve my writing, Amanda, Velia, and Lauren, thank you for your valuable feedback and suggestions. You have made this book better with your keen eyes and sharp minds. I appreciate your honesty and your friendship.

To my sister and illustrator, Flora, for lending me her time and talent. You have brought my words to life with your beautiful illustration. I thank you for your creativity and generosity. You are a gifted artist and a wonderful sister.

To my mother and my three sisters, for their relentless support and encouragement. You have always believed in me and cheered me on. I admire your strength and your love.

To my talented photographer, Tony, who always works wonders. You are a master of your craft and a great person.

And to my husband, David, who has been my rock and my light throughout this journey. You have supported me in every way possible, and encouraged me to pursue my passion. You are my best friend and my soulmate. I am beyond grateful for your love.

NOTES

PART 1: YOUR EARS AREN'T THAT BIG
It all depends on how you look at things

3. Roses are Red, Violets are Bold
Sciencing, "Colors of the Rainbow," Sciencing, April 24, 2017, https://sciencing.com/colors-rainbow-8388948.html
Cowley, L. (n.d.). Primary rainbow: Colors. Atmospheric Optics. https://www.atoptics.co.uk/rainbows/primcol.htm
Quantum Stones. (2016, June 13). The power and meaning of colors: Exploring the rainbow of life. QuantumStones.com. https://quantumstones.com/the-power-and-meaning-of-colors-exploring-the-rainbow-of-life/

4. Are you a Mountain or an Old Goat?
McCartney, P. (1968). Hey Jude [Song]. On The Beatles. Apple.

5. If it Walks Like a Duck
Robert Quackenbush (1978), Henry's Awful Mistake (New York: Parents' Magazine Press).

6. Deflecting Big Lips
BetterHelp. (2020, June 8). What is deflection?
Psychology explains this defense mechanism.
BetterHelp
https://www.betterhelp.com/advice/psychologists/wh
at-is-deflection-psychology-explains-this-defense-
mechanism/#Common%20Underlying%20Themes
%20of%20Deflection
American Psychological Association. (2016,
December 13). True Lies: People Who Lie Via
Telling Truth Viewed Harshly, Study Finds [Press
release].
https://www.apa.org/news/press/releases/2016/12/tr
ue-lies

11. Just Spray and Walk Away –
Peggy Trowbridge Filippone, "The Benefits of Slow
Cooker Cooking," The Spruce Eats, Dotdash,
updated February 24, 2020, 1.

12. You Look Just Like Your Father, He was an
Ugly Man
Rumi. (2004). When our crowns go crooked. (C.
Barks, Trans.). In The essential Rumi (p. 123).
HarperOne.

13. Scales and Mirrors
Glossyfied. (2022, November 6). Why do I look
different in different mirrors? 9.
https://www.glossyfied.com/why-do-i-look-different-
in-different-mirrors/

James Clear, Atomic Habits: An Easy & Proven Way to Build Good Habits & Break Bad Ones (New York: Avery, 2018).

PART 2: HE LOVES ME, HE LOVES ME NOT
Love Yourself

14. He Loves Me, He Loves Me Not
Waddle, C., & Rylands, K. (2019). Understanding & building confidence (2nd ed.). Confidence Books.
Barton Goldsmith, "When You Give Love Freely, It Returns to You," Psychology Today, Sussex Publishers, May 8, 2019, https://www.psychologytoday.com/us/blog/emotional-fitness/201905/when-you-give-love-freely-it-returns-to-you.

15. Running Around Circles
Buckminster Fuller Institute, "Home," Buckminster Fuller Institute, https://www.bfi.org/.
Special Collections and University Archives, "R. Buckminster Fuller timeline," R. Buckminster Fuller Collection, Stanford University Libraries, https://exhibits.stanford.edu/bucky/feature/r-buckminster-fuller-timeline.

16. Take Your Worries and Stuff 'em in a Box
Backus, Bertha Adams. "The Laugh." The Poetry of Bertha Adams Backus, edited by John Smith, 2nd ed., Oxford UP, 2020, pp. 45-46.
Wignall, N. (2018, April 20). Why we worry (and how

to stop). Nick Wignall. https://nickwignall.com/why-we-worry/.
Wignall, Nick. "4 Things Emotionally Intelligent People Don't Do." Nick Wignall, 4 Apr. 2020, https://nickwignall.com/emotionally-intelligent-people/.

17. Eating Rocks
Buehler, J. (2019, February 1). Alligators gobble rocks to stay underwater longer. Science. 9. https://www.sciencemag.org/news/2019/02/alligators-gobble-rocks-stay-underwater-longer

19. When You're Done, You're Done
Smith, Kathleen, PhD, LPC (2020, February 21). The Psychology of Dealing With Change: How to Become Resilient. PSYCOM https://www.psycom.net/dealing-with-change

20. Well of Wealth
Rath, T. (2007). Strengths finder 2.0. New York, Gallup Press
Rath, T. (2007). Now, discover your strengths. Gallup Press

21. Finding Our Feathers
https://blog.nature.org/science/2015/09/28/angry-birds-molting-grumpy-science/
https://www.finefeatherheads.com/the-meaning-of-white-black-and-grey-feathers-a-message-from-the-divine/

24. When Life Lacks Luster
https://spaceplace.nasa.gov/what-is-gravity/en/#Gravity%20in%20Our%20Universe
25. Flap Your Wings and Take a Power Nap
https://chipperbirds.com/do-birds-get-tired-of-flying/
www.jamesmaas.com/
Harold Garza, (Feb. 13, 2012). Slumberwise
https://slumberwise.com/health/siesta-the-little-nap-with-a-big-history/

26. Painting Over Walls and Your Ex's Tattoo
TALK ART -
https://podcasts.apple.com/gb/podcast/lily-van-der-stokker/id1439567112?i=1000559777520
ARTNET.COM – https://news.artnet.com/art-world/indonesia-pig-art-oldest-painting-1937110
REMOVERY.COM
https://removery.com/blog/ex-name-tattoo-cover-up/

PART 3: RUNNING THROUGH SPRIKLERS
Connecting with Others

29. Keep Your Pants to Yourself
Author and Rest Coach, Octavia Raheem
https://www.octaviaraheem.com/

30. Running the Mile-y Cyrus
Cyrus, Miley. "Used To Be Young." Endless Summer Vacation, RCA, 2023, CD.

35. Holy Guacamole
Eding, J., & Ellis, D. (2009). How to hug a porcupine: Easy ways to love the difficult people in your life. Hatherleigh Press.

36. Name Your Pillar
Bandillo, T. (2022). The secrets of Solomon's pillars. HarperCollins. https://doi.org/10.1000/182

ABOUT THE AUTHOR

Rosa Valle-Lopez is a veteran television news journalist, who has worked for NBC and CBS affiliate stations in Los Angeles. She spent three decades in the trenches of a newsroom, witnessing and reporting on world-changing events, gaining insights into the human condition and the ways we can support and inspire each other. She uses humor and personal anecdotes to share quirky life lessons. She has received numerous acknowledgments for her work, including Los Angeles Area Emmy and Los Angeles Golden Mike awards. She is an avid supporter of community and nonprofit work. Rosa is the mother of three and lives in Southern California with her husband, David. You can read more of her stories at [www.wordpaddle.com]

www.ingramcontent.com/pod-product-compliance
Lightning Source LLC
Chambersburg PA
CBHW022338280326
41934CB00006B/684